The Postnational Constellation

Books by Jürgen Habermas included in the series
Studies in Contemporary German Social Thought
Thomas McCarthy, general editor

The Postnational Constellation

Political Essays

Jürgen Habermas

Translated, edited and with an introduction
by Max Pensky

The MIT Press

Cambridge, Massachusetts

• **Postnational Constellation:**
First MIT Press edition, 2001
This translation © 2001 Polity Press
First published in Germany as *Die postnationale Konstellation: Politische Essays*
© 1998 Suhrkamp Verlag

Library of Congress Cataloging-in-Publication Data

Habermas, Jürgen.
   [Postnationale Konstellation. English]
   The postnational constellation: political essays / Jürgen Habermas; translated, edited, and with an introduction by Max Pensky.—1st MIT Press ed.
     p. cm.—(Studies in contemporary German social thought)
   Includes bibliographical references and index.
   ISBN 0-262-08297-7 (hc.: alk. paper)—ISBN 0-262-58206-6 (pbk.: alk. paper)
     1. National state. 2. Democracy. 3. World politics—1989– I. Pensky, Max, 1961– II. Title. III. Series.

JC311. H32 2001
320.1'01—dc21

                                         00-048963

Typeset in 11 on 13 pt Berling
by Kolam Information Services Private Limited, Pondicherry, India.
Printed in Great Britain by MPG Books Ltd, Bodmin, Cornwall

This book is printed on acid-free paper.

Contents

Acknowledgements

The publishers wish to thank the following for permission to use copyright material:

Blätter Verlagsgesellschaft mbH, Bonn for Habermas, 'How to Learn from History', translated by Max Pensky, *Blätter für deutsche und internationale Politik* 42 (1997), pp. 408–16.

Modern Schoolman for Habermas, 'Remarks on Legitimation through Human Rights', translated by William Rehg, *Modern Schoolman*, 75:2 (1998).

Every effort has been made to trace the copyright holders but if any have been inadvertently overlooked the publishers will be pleased to make the necessary arrangement at the first opportunity.

Editor's Introduction

I

"Globalization": the term has become indispensable – and unavoidable – for a spectrum of current debates from political economy and democracy, law and human rights to cultural controversies over identity and difference. It seems to be a term destined to provoke only ambiguous reactions. On the one hand, "globalization" evokes the image of proliferating interconnections and interrelationship, of better communication between the most far-flung regions of the world, challenging old prejudices and pointing toward a future where the cultural, geographical, and political sources of social conflicts have become antiques. On the other hand, it calls forth panic-tinged images of global markets running out of control, of an unguided and uncontrollable acceleration of modernization processes, devastating the political infrastructures of nation-states and leaving them increasingly unable to manage their economies – and the social and ecological crises they generate. On the one hand, globalization hints at the utopian vision of once-hostile strangers coming into peaceable contact through globalized media of all kinds; on the other hand, it hints at the dystopian specter of forced cultural homogenization either by the decrees of a centralized administration or by market fiat – for developing countries, the eradication of the sources of any cultural identities unconducive to the mandatory, market-driven adaptation to Western-style modes of life, to be replaced only by the bland Americanization of a global consumer culture; for Europe, a bureaucratically imposed, standardized Euroculture offered as the regulatory compensation for obsolete national characters, which live on only in the pallid form of commodities for mass tourism. Finally, perhaps the most glaring and disturbing either/or: "globalization" as the last, mutedly triumphant stage in the halting and frequently derailed process of global political democratization that began with the revolutionary introduction of the principles of popular sovereignty at the end of the eighteenth century – globalization, in other words, as a staggering (in both senses) crossing of the finish line that also makes a bit more plausible the hope that a global democracy could be institutionalized with sufficient strength and sensitivity that global crises of war, injustice and inequity, and ecological devastation could become themes for a worldwide democratic process. Or: "globalization" as that market-driven homogenizing, dominating force that reveals precisely how thin the basis of legitimacy for democratic processes actually is within the current constellation of nation-states; globalization as the end of democratization – not as its culmination but as the defining feature of the historical epoch marking the end of the national-state model for the institution of democracy. Thus globalization pointing (maybe not all that dimly) toward a future where global political and social decisions rest on the only structures capable of accommodating their complexity: highly evolved administrative state mechanisms, and highly dynamic and flexible markets, both of which operate much more efficiently by regarding their populations as clients or customers, and largely dispense with the direct participation of citizens. Mustering these conflicting images, fears, and hopes is not so difficult. Finding a way to sort them out, to confront their ambiguity squarely, and to shed some explanatory light on them – to analyze them as challenges, rather than as overwhelming fate – is not so easy. But this is the task that Jürgen Habermas sets for himself in *The Postnational Constellation*.

Since the middle of the twentieth century, Jürgen Habermas has been among the most vocal and influential advocates for an unashamed universalism in political and moral questions. His sprawling theoretical work, from his theory of rationality, through a theory of "discourse ethics" to a theory of law and democracy, is unified by the simple (and correspondingly ambitious) task of demonstrating that the range of universalistic intuitions in morality, politics, and law – the heritage of the eighteenth-century Enlightenment – is no mere projection of power or local preference. Instead, Habermas argues that universality is embedded in the most basic capacities that we possess as persons capable of speaking, hearing, giving and accepting reasons for our actions, and conducting our lives correspondingly. In the most fundamental and distinctive human capacity – the ability to speak to one another, to decide on the basis of reasons and arguments, to distinguish between understanding and deception – Habermas insists we find a universal, if modest, basis for the great political innovations of popular sovereignty, legally enforceable human rights, democratic procedures, and the inconspicuous but vital solidarity that binds humans together, and makes them accountable to one another, through the mutual recognition of the status of personhood. The central claim of Habermas's theories is that the institutions based on the communicative use of human reason, from our moral intuitions to the institutions of the democratic constitutional state under the rule of law, are reasonable, and not merely the contingent consequences of historical circumstances.

Given Habermas's theoretical commitment to this claim to universality, one might have expected his frequent political interventions to carry on, in concrete terms, his larger theoretical ambitions, and indeed any reader familiar with Habermas's theoretical work will find in the essays collected in *The Postnational Constellation* a clear relation to the theoretical defense of universalism. But to Habermas's credit – and no other fact speaks more forcefully to the current relevance and ongoing importance of Habermas's work as a public intellectual – his theory is never simply imposed on his occasional writings; indeed, for a prodigious theory-writer, Habermas has never fallen into the trap of making the facts fit the theory. While intimately involved with his theoretical ambitions, Habermas's political writings carry on a noticeably tense relation with them.

Political developments certainly can and often do disappoint universalist expectations, and in this sense a universalist position in politics and morality can at the very least provide a vocabulary to make clear why the costs of globalization – missed opportunities for popular political participation, for example, or exacerbated social inequities, or the loss of culture – can be registered as "costs" in a normative, and not merely in a value-neutral, sense. In their complexity and persistence, however, political and social crises also challenge the theoretical position itself, urging the theoretical clarification of "our" universalistic normative intuitions toward a heightened degree of self-criticism, openness, and flexibility.

The resulting dialectic between universalist theory and pointedly particular and up-to-date political writing is nowhere more clear than here, where Habermas confronts the ambiguous consequences of globalization in their full range. Rather than take the simple step of emphasizing the "good," universalistic reading of globalization, the essays collected here derive much of their value from their unflinching analyses of the "bad"; including the real possibility that the bad might win, all our universalistic sympathies notwithstanding. That globalization *ought* to be the harbinger for a renewed impulse toward global democracy and human rights is uncontested. That market-driven globalization processes in themselves will provide such an impetus, however, is a highly questionable assertion which no amount of theoretical commitment by itself will decide. Following the arguments presented in *The Postnational Constellation* does not require any particular expertise in Habermas's theories; in fact, taken together they provide a lucid and concise political introduction to why, now more than ever, a broadly ambitious but realistic and flexible theoretical explanation of the ambiguities of social modernization has become indispensable.

II

This latest installment in a series of political essays dating back to the 1950s nevertheless marks a decisive break from Habermas's previous writings as a public intellectual, as the title already announces. For over forty years, Jürgen Habermas has been one of the most influential and astute observers of the political developments of the Federal Republic of Germany. In a strong sense, indeed, Habermas has been *the* intellectual figure of the Federal Republic, not just because of the broad influence of his theoretical work in the academic world, but through the depth of his engagement with Germany's ongoing task of developing a political culture of freedom and democracy from the ashes of the Second World War and history's unparalleled moral and political catastrophe. The political and social consequences of that catastrophe for Germany – a divided nation, and a decidedly mixed role as a political and ideological focal point of the Cold War – contain, in miniature, virtually all of the crisis tendencies of postwar Europe. For the unified Federal Republic of Germany, however, the political history of the postwar era continues to reverberate in contemporary debates over nationhood, the role of the state, and the bases of democratic legitimacy. Because pre-unification West Germany's postwar "Basic Law" was imposed by the Allied powers without any popular referendum, the Federal Republic of Germany found itself in the unparalleled situation of standing under a strikingly liberal political constitution without any corresponding basis in a liberal political culture. Much of the political-cultural history of that nation, then, consisted in the unique task of growing a political culture to match institutions already in place. This fact certainly explains Habermas's understandable concern with the "bases of legitimacy" for the democratic process. It also underlies his unwavering attention to the unstable relationship between the democratic process and "the nation," understood as a pre-political form of collective association based on the supposedly organic categories of language, shared history, or common culture. The rhetoric of nationalism – in itself the perfect contradictory to universalism, as it is based virtually entirely on acts of exclusion – was effective in justifying Germany's descent into fascism; for Habermas nothing is more painfully characteristic of the pitfalls of modernization – and the ambiguities and tensions of globalization – than the fact that global problems and challenges frequently provoke renewed forms of nationalism as their response.

Habermas's role as an engaged public intellectual in the political public sphere of the Federal Republic of Germany has largely consisted in helping to cultivate a "postconventional," post-nationalist, post-particularist political culture, in which the abstract principles of mutual recognition, collective will-formation, and popular sovereignty expressed in the constitution and in the political infrastructure could acquire a broader basis in the attitudes and feelings of citizens. He has been an unflagging critic of any efforts to "renationalize" Germany's political life: he bitterly opposed neoconservative efforts to relativize and lessen the unique burden of moral reflection imposed on Germany by the Holocaust, efforts that culminated in the debacle at Bitburg. He was a harsh critic of the cynical appeals to national feeling that the Kohl administration used to grease the skids of a largely bureaucratically managed unification of Germany, and he fought against the nationalist-inspired sleight-of-hand used to tighten the Federal Republic's liberal immigration and asylum laws by constitutional means. He has continued to be the most forceful and eloquent spokesperson for a conception of "constitutional patriotism" – a sense of shared identity based on the abstract principles of democratic procedure contained in the Federal Republic's Basic Law, and against all efforts to "substantialize" Germany's political culture by any uncritical reappropriation of naturalized categories of nation, language, culture, shared ethnicity, and so on.

All of this, of course, is not without a certain irony: in his passionate defense of a post-traditional, post-nationalist conception of Germany, Habermas had remained, predominantly, a *German* intellectual, in the sense that his universalistic interventions remained intimately tied to the particular issues and problems of his own country. As a moral and political principle, Habermas recognizes, universalism can only be plausibly realized through the very particular history, traditions, and forms of life that continue to characterize national cultures, even as those national cultures begin to buckle under the pressure of social, economic, and political globalization processes.

And this is where the essays collected in this volume mark a decisive turning point for Habermas's role as a politically engaged public intellectual. Rather than mobilizing universalistic orientations and arguments to address specifically German issues and problems, Habermas reverses himself: now German history and specifically German experiences serve pedagogically to provide some instruction about problems that have, like it or not, become global. Globalization has also globalized the political public spheres of citizens, and has thus globalized the focus of public intellectuals operating within those public spheres as well. The end of the nation-state also obliges intellectuals to "universalize" themselves, their subjects, and their audiences, in an unprecedented way.

The dynamic of globalization, ambiguous as it may be, is for Habermas reasonably clear in one respect: it heralds the end of the global dominance of the nation-state as a model for political organization. "Postnational" here means that the globalization of markets and of economic processes generally, of modes of communication and commerce, of culture, and of risk, all increasingly deprive the classical nation-state of its formerly assured bases of sovereign power, which it depended on to fulfill its equally classic functions: to secure peace internally and defend its borders abroad, to set fair conditions for a domestic market economy and to exert what influence it can on domestic markets via macroeconomic policies, to raise taxes and allocate budgets to assure the maintenance of a minimum social standard and the redress of social inequities, to enforce individual rights and take measures to secure conditions for their effective realization. By undermining each and every one of these capacities, Habermas argues, globalization fundamentally challenges the relevance of the nation-state as a continued political model.

Hence the ambiguity of globalization. Market- and technology-driven processes undermine the stability of a form of political organization that itself is, from a normative point of view, incapable of being harmonized with basic universalistic principles: the nation-state is fading, and a good thing too. But at the same time, there is no guarantee that the nation-state will be replaced by anything better. Globalization processes themselves offer few clues about how the basis of legitimacy for democratic processes can be broadened, in a postnational world, beyond the partial (and in a sense conceptually incoherent) particularist bases that nation-states have so far been able to generate. Taken as a whole, the central essays in *The Postnational Constellation* all respond to this ambiguous situation with an unambiguous message: if the democratic process is to secure a basis for legitimacy beyond the nation-state, then neither state structures nor market mechanisms, but popular processes of collective will-formation alone will have to provide it. Bureaucratic initiatives and market dynamics may succeed in palliating some of the harshest crises that arise from modernization processes. But only effective popular sovereignty – subsisting in transnational networks of communication, in the proliferation of interconnected public spheres, in cooperative non-governmental organizations, in popular political movements with a global outlook – will be able to generate a mode of popular legitimacy broad and strong enough to enable transnational, regional, or global political regimes to carry out binding political decisions and enforce binding social policies. Social solidarity, in other words, which like it or not can no longer coherently subsist within the particular perspective of nation-states, will have to take a further "abstractive step." As opposed both to the administrative state and to global markets, solidarity will have to emerge as a truly cosmopolitan phenomenon; a global sense of shared responsibility and shared commitments to inclusion and participation will have to develop in the effective attitudes of citizens of the world, if democracy is to survive the demise of the nation-state.

Such a call for a "compulsory" cosmopolitan solidarity, beyond the affective ties of nation, language, place, and heritage, may itself sound hopelessly abstract, and Habermas harbors no naive hopes concerning the difficulty of shifting popular sentiments of inclusion, belonging, and shared interests to such a thin atmosphere. But the difficulty, he insists, is itself an empirical matter and not one of principle, and will thus have to be tested in the choppy political waters of the postnational constellation, rather than dismissed out of hand. Cosmopolitan solidarity is itself nothing other than the mode of sociality

demanded by the abstract constitutional principles of equal
freedom for all under equal rights, the principles that democratic constitutional nation-states themselves rest on.

III

And here the lessons of German history can help illuminate the
pitfalls and potentials of such a project. The first essay of this
collection analyses intellectual aspects of the German *Vormärz*
(literally, the period of republican foment in German history
from 1815 to the failed republican revolution in March 1848)
in which German intellectuals struggled to find a vocabulary for
appropriating the "ideals of 1789" in the politically and culturally fragmented German context. By focussing on the "Assembly of the Germanists," in 1846, Habermas shows how German
intellectuals were simultaneously energized by the universalizing dynamic of the principles of popular sovereignty, and
hobbled by the belief that the realization of such principles
could only come about in a political environment defined by
"the nation" as the expression of a *Volk*, a people with a pre-
political, organic form of shared identity rooted in place, descent, and language. The conceptual incoherence of this belief,
which Habermas teases out of the details of the protocols and
proceedings of the convention itself, would have enormous
consequences, both for the immediate future of German republicanism and for the subsequent train of catastrophes that mark
modern German political history. The myth of the "organic"
nation turns out, consistently, to be the product of a concerted
effort at historiographical construction – and historical fantasy.
In the end, such a belief in the supposed need for a scholarly
recovery of "national identity" or "the spirit of a people," which
German historians, legal scholars, and philologists understood
as their special responsibility, proves impossible to reconcile
with the *construction* of a constitutional regime based on citizens who live under equal freedom and equal rights. The second essay here, "On the Public Use of History," reprints
Habermas's controversial defense of Daniel Goldhagen's

Hitler's Willing Executioners, a book whose startlingly simple thesis – Germans committed the Holocaust because they were anti-Semites through and though, in a way different from any other European society – sparked bitter debates in a newly united Germany still struggling with the use or abuse of its recent history. Habermas's essay shows the persistence, and the persistent attraction, of the belief that professional history has a special responsibility to intervene in public debates over collective identity, on behalf of a sense of national belonging based on approved history. The role of historians as uncritical caretakers of national heritage as a source of national health, like the notion of scholars as nation-builders in general, Habermas implies, is an especially poor one for any country wishing to engage in a critical collective dialogue over its collective past, and to move forward with any deserved confidence into its political future.

Taken together these two essays on "the national context" draw lessons for the challenge of globalization. The next three essays apply them to the contemporary world situation. "Learning from Catastrophe?" paints in broad strokes the trends and tendencies that have culminated in the current political constellation, and crystallizes in the call for a new mode of solidarity beyond the nation-state if the crisis tendencies of the twentieth century are to be made into resources for collective learning, rather than omens for the return of old catastrophes.

At the heart of this collection, the long essay on "The Postnational Constellation and the Future of Democracy" spells out Habermas's position in detail. I have already provided some introductory summary of the themes and arguments of this essay, which clearly stands as one of Habermas's most significant and sweeping analyses of the contemporary political scene.

The fifth essay, "Remarks on Legitimation through Human Rights," provides some fine-tuning of one of the basic arguments of the collection, the current political challenge of shifting the basis of legitimacy for constitutional democracies onto the level of abstract principles. The sixth, "Conceptions of Modernity," provides a sweeping overview of the development of conceptions of rationality and reason in modern philosophy and sociology, demonstrating how the project of providing a theory of modernity through the means of a critique of reason became bogged down into conceptual dead ends, which Habermas traces to contemporary postmodern theory. By situating his own conception of a discourse model of human reason as a plausible way out of this dead end, the essay also illuminates the internal connections between Habermas's theory of rationality and his political diagnoses.

The final section of the volume collects some of Habermas's occasional pieces; his brief contributions to the ongoing debate on the ethics of human cloning, in particular, show how moral intuitions must constantly work to keep pace with technological change.

Chapter 5, "Remarks on Legitimation through Human Rights," was translated by William Rehg. The translation of chapter 3, "Learning from Catastrophe? A Look Back at the Short Twentieth Century," is based on an earlier translation by Hella Beister. The translation of chapter 6, "Conceptions of Modernity: A Look Back at Two Traditions," is based on an earlier English version by Professor Habermas. My thanks to Peter Gilgen at Cornell University for consultation, and Lynn Dunlop at Polity Press.

Foreword

"Flow and boundary" – a suggestive image for a new constellation of border crossings. The Frankfurt "Assembly of the Germanists" of 1846 set out to construct national borders; today those same borders are increasingly fading away. The two introductory essays to this volume illuminate German nationhood from two mutually opposed perspectives. The Germanists of the mid-nineteenth century looked out upon the nation's republican beginnings; today we look back somberly at its catastrophic end.[1]

The diagnostic retrospective on the short twentieth century is an attempt to explain the feeling of enlightened helplessness that seems to predominate in these times, and to direct our attention to a genuinely disturbing problem that we will all face in the coming century: can democracies based on the social-welfare state survive beyond national borders? The title essay of this volume explores the alternatives to the dominant neo-liberal positions – and dispenses with any naive trust in the rhetoric of a "third way" beyond neoliberalism and social democracy.[2]

A unified European monetary policy marks the beginning of a reversal of old alliances: satisfied Market Europeans have now formed common cause with nationalistic Euroskeptics to freeze the status quo of an economically integrated but still politically fragmented Europe. But the price for this status quo is paid in the coin of growing social inequities. It is a price that is almost certainly too high, according to the standards of civility that we have already achieved. In the current context, the claim that democratic legitimacy cannot be secured without social justice has itself become a conservative principle. However dubious the utopian fantasies of both the Left and the Right have become, it is clear that "revolutionaries" and "conservatives" have exchanged roles: a "revolutionary" attempt is underway to defamiliarize the population with the standards of egalitarian universalism, and to trace socially generated inequities back to the natural characteristics of "winners" and "losers."

In the national context, of course, it is harder than ever for politics to keep pace with global competition. I see the only normatively satisfactory alternative as a socially and economically effective European Union, constituted along federalist lines – an alternative that points to a future cosmopolitan order sensitive both to difference and to social equality. Only a Europe in which the domestication of violence engages each and every form of society and culture would be immune from the postcolonial relapse into Eurocentrism. And an intercultural discourse on human rights provides the terms in which a truly decentered perspective must prove itself.

The final three chapters provide a rough sketch of the philosophical background for my analyses of the challenges of the postnational constellation in the volume's central section. Finally, a concept of autonomy that lies at the heart of the self-understanding of modernity forms the basis for an argument against human cloning.

J.H.
Starnberg, June 1998

1

What is a People?

The Frankfurt "Germanists' Assembly" of 1846 and the Self-Understanding of the Humanities in the *Vormärz*

I. Dual Objectives

The dual objectives that the organizers of the "Germanists' assembly" had in mind can be seen clearly enough, both from the letter of invitation "to an assembly of scholars at Frankfurt a.M.", as well as the short introductory text to the *Proceedings of the Germanists*,[1] the assembly's official record. On the initiative of the Tübingen jurist Reycher, prominent scholars such as Jacob and Wilhelm Grimm, Georg Gottfried Gervinus, Leopold Ranke, Ludwig Uhland, Friedrich Christoph Dahlmann, Georg Beseler, and Karl Mittermaier gathered with the goal of founding a union of the three disciplines of German law, German history, and German language. Their primary objective was the institutionalization of an improved mode of scholarly and professional communication. Until that time, any professional exchanges beyond the normal medium of books and newspapers depended entirely on personal acquaintance and correspondence. This was true not just for interdisciplinary communication between jurists, linguists, and historians, but also for communication within the disciplines themselves,

Address for the Centenary celebration of the Johann Wolfgang Goethe-Universität, Frankfurt/Main particularly among German philologists. There was thus a keenly felt need for more robust forms of personal contact, for mutual understanding and learning – "in free speech and unforced conversation" and "without prepared lectures." The earliest German disciplinary congresses of physicians and natural scientists (beginning in 1822), and classical philologists (beginning in 1838), served as preliminary models. The organizers of the Germanists' assembly were, of course, well aware that a collective assembly of Germanistic scholars would itself be understood as a political act.

The second objective went beyond any disciplinary needs. It was to stage a subtle demonstration on behalf of the unification of a politically fragmented Fatherland:

> It would be asking too much of a meeting of scholars if...its goal were to be set as the direct intervention in life; yet we expect no mean task from this assembly if, standing on a firm foundation of scholarly research, it acknowledges both the importance and the gravity of these times, and will satisfy, for each individual, the enthusiasm that animates us all.[2]

The course of the assembly itself would confirm this expectation. Re-reading these protocols, even those of us in later generations, who feel bound through profession and biography both to the humanities and to the republican traditions of this country, can sense the strength of emotion that had moved these speakers. In hindsight, of course, we can also recognize the unpolitical dimension in the passions of these heroes of the German Historical School. Nevertheless, no amount of criticism can entirely remove the peculiar charm of these voices, animated as they are by the spirit of Romanticism. Their interest in "Germanic antiquities," the objects of their work, coincides in a virtually unconscious way with the political tendencies of their times.

The assembly itself is surely colored by a tragic irony: what was celebrated so enthusiastically as a new beginning signified, in objective terms, an end as well – both politically and in the history of the humanities. The assemblies of the Germanists, in Frankfurt in 1846 and in Lübeck the following year, constituted both the first and the last attempts to unify the three disciplines that had formed the core of the early humanities. Fifteen years later, both the German jurists and the German philologists would found their own independent associations, entirely in keeping with the normal differentiation of scholarly disciplines.

From the end of the eighteenth century, new humanistic disciplines had arisen alongside the older, established fields such as classical philology or art history. Initially, at least, a common basis of shared historicist convictions had kept these new disciplines from separating from one another; they were still far more than mere background environments for each other. But this early period was already nearing its end in the 1840s. Among the participants in the 1846 Germanists' assembly, we find only four of the figures that the historian Erich Rothacker counts among the founding fathers of the humanities in Germany: Jacob and Wilhelm Grimm, Leopold Ranke, and Friedrich Gottlieb Welcker. They are the last in the illustrious line of Herder, Möser, Wolf, Friedrich and August Wilhelm Schlegel, Schleiermacher, Humboldt, Niebuhr, Savigny, Eichhorn, Creuzer, Görres, Bopp, and Boeckh.[3] Rothacker sets the parameters for this founding phase, during which the different scholarly disciplines still spoke a common language, with two famous quotations from the eighty-year period between 1774 and 1854: "Every nation contains its own central point of felicity, just as every sphere has its center of gravity" (Herder); "Every epoch stands in an immediate relation to God, and its value lies not in what it produces, but in its existence itself" (Ranke). The Frankfurt assembly, which sought to open a new chapter in the history of the humanistic sciences, actually marked the end of this founding period. Seen from the perspective of the history of the humanities, it was exactly suited for such a *translatio nominis*; indeed at that time the honorary title of "Germanist," which Jacob Grimm had claimed for linguistics alone, was also entering into general usage by legal historians and modern philologists.[4]

The role that the Germanists believed they could play as the natural interpreters of the spirit of the people in the political public sphere proved equally illusory. As is well known, two years after the Frankfurt assembly, the attempt in the neighboring *Paulskirche* to achieve national unification through a liberal constitution ended in failure. Roughly 10 percent of the participants in the Germanists' assembly met once again in the first German National Assembly in 1848, most of them as centrists. Wilhelm Scherer would later describe the Germanists' assembly as "a sort of precursor to the Frankfurt parliament."[5] The *Vormärz* period was both the first and the last time that leading representatives of the humanities possessed the political will to make public use of their professional knowledge as intellectuals and citizens. What could still appear in my own teachers' generation – before, during, and after 1933 – as an attempt to exercise a political and intellectual influence obviously does not fall into this category of civil engagement. The role of intellectuals is utterly dependent on the sounding board of a liberal public sphere and a political culture grounded in freedom. With their demands for freedom of the press, the Germanists in the Frankfurt *Kaisersaal* 150 years ago understood this clearly. One cannot say the same of Julius Petersen, Alfred Bäumler, Ernst Bertram, Hans Naumann, or Erich Rothacker.

The *Paulskirche* movement failed due to historical circumstances that are not my theme here. But the Germanists, who are of interest to me as a part of this movement, did not fail due to external circumstances alone. A political self-understanding that was shaped by the philosophy of the early humanities was also a decisive factor. There was, first, the desire to place themselves beyond any disciplinary boundaries, no matter how rapidly and clearly those boundaries emerged. But equally problematic was the unselfconscious fabrication of political relationships based on shared descent, which were intended to give the German nation the appearance of a natural phenomenon. Following the lead of Jacob Grimm, I will briefly sketch the philosophical background of the Historical School (II). I will use the contradictions that emerge from this sketch to show how the idea of a "spirit of the people," a *Volksgeist*, always directed toward a real or imagined past, poses insurmountable difficulties for the future-oriented intentions of liberal republicanism (III). Gervinus avoids the fatal dialectic of inclusion and exclusion through a historically dynamic reading of the doctrine of the spirit of the people. But at that time, it was only democrats who remained unrepresented in the Germanists' assembly, people such as Julius Fröbel, who were willing to pay attention the precarious relationship between the culturally defined "people" and the "nation" of citizens (IV). I will conclude by recalling the factors internal to scholarly disciplines themselves that disposed the Germanists to an unpolitical self-understanding.

II.   The Worldview of the Early Humanities

Jacob Grimm officially opened the second public session of the assembly with remarks on the relation between the natural and the human sciences. Chemistry and physics served as examples of exact sciences based on calculation, which conceive of nature as a mechanism, deconstructing it into its component parts and reassembling it for technical objectives. The "inexact" sciences, on the other hand, operate quite differently, thanks to a finely developed and highly sensitive disposition ("a rare device of exceptional natures") for penetrating into the organic multiplicity and interiority of the historical creations of humankind. The human sciences are not characterized by the "levers and contraptions that awe and astonish the human race," but rather through the inherent worth, the dignity of their objects: "That which is human, whether in language, poetry, law, or history, is closer to our hearts than animals, plants, or elements.... It is with the same weapons," Grimm concludes with a startlingly militant turn of phrase, "that the nation triumphs over all that is foreign."[6]

At the heart of this elliptical formulation is the claim that the observational and explanatory natural sciences encompass general phenomena and lawlike states of affairs, while the human sciences, based on understanding, are dedicated to the cultural uniqueness and the distinctive individuality of their objects. Grimm had more in mind than the contradiction between general and particular, between "nomothetic" and "ideographic" science, as Windelband would later describe them. He relates this contradiction to the contrast between the foreign and the familiar, and thereby sharpens a hermeneutical claim concerning the prejudicial structure of understanding, according to which we understand what is closest to us better than what is foreign. Like must be recognized by like. This is most evident in poetry, which "can in reality only be understood in the mother tongue," as well as "Germanic antiquities." Understanding such historical documents of the "spirit of a people" is no neutral scientific operation; it is deeply rooted in feeling. To understand truly is to bring the whole of one's subjectivity into play, a process of recognition whose ultimate goal is the enthusiastic moment of self-recognition in the other. Hermeneutical understanding appears to live from the pathos of appropriation:

> The chemical crucible will come to a boil under *any* flame; newly discovered plants, baptized in cold Latin, will grow in any *similar* climate *everywhere*; but we are better pleased by the unearthing of a long-lost word of German than by the rediscovery of a *foreign* one, because we can reappropriate it into our own country: every discovery in the history of the Fatherland directly benefits the Fatherland itself.[7]

For Jacob Grimm, the inclusive character of scientific and scholarly communication itself leads beyond the cool universalism of the natural sciences: "The exact sciences encompass the whole earth, and foreign scholars stand to benefit from them as well. But they do not seize the heart."[8] The human sciences, by contrast, are so deeply embedded in their own respective cultures that their results are of interest primarily to members of those cultures. The "German sciences" are thus addressed to a German public.[9]

The spirit of a people, which provides the ultimate referent for this differentiation between the familiar and the foreign, expresses itself most purely in its poetry. And this, in turn, is immediately connected with a "native language." Jacob Grimm could thus answer the apparently simple question, "What is a people?" with the claim that "a people is the essence of all those who speak the same language."[10] Despite what appears at first glance to be a purely culturalistic determination, "a people" is thus reformulated in substantialist terms. It is no coincidence that all the metaphors for language, in which the spirit of the people expresses itself, are borrowed from natural history and biology.

As Jacob's brother Wilhelm Grimm reported to the assembly on the collective project of the *Dictionary of the German Language*, he described the cultural desolation in the wake of the Thirty Years War with the imagery of a natural landscape and its flora:

> Language too, wilted and the leaves fell one by one from the boughs...at the beginning of the eighteenth century, dark clouds still hung over the ancient trees, whose life force seemed to have all but vanished...only Goethe's staff, striking the face of the cliff, let loose a fresh spring to stream over the barren drought lands; once again they turned to green, and the spring flowers of poetry appeared anew.[11]

This organic vision of language, in turn, implies a protective role for the caretakers of language. Their defensive attacks against foreign admixtures are intended to purify their native tongue without putting it in the chains of standardization.

> Do not think that the Dictionary, because it undertakes the historical transformation of language, shall for that reason also prove itself to be casual or lenient. It will rebuke all that which has unjustly penetrated, even if some of it must be patiently borne; because in every language there will be individual shoots that grow poor and deformed, and which can no longer be weeded out.[12]

Whoever uses a naturalized conception of language as a definition of a people and its spirit needs to delimit the nation unambiguously in time and space: "Our forbears were Germans, even before they were converted to Christianity; it is an *ancient* estate, which forms the point of departure for all of us, a condition that has unified us, one with the other, into a bond as Germans."[13] This continuity of the spirit of the people, grounded in the history of its language, endows the *Volksnation*, the nation of the people, with a quality of naturalness or organicity. But once the nation is conceived as organic, the project of

national unification loses its constructive character as the production of a modern nation of citizens. And what is true of
duration in time is also true of extension in space: if the nation
is, or ought to be, coextensive with a linguistic community,
then the contingent borders of national territories vanish in the
face of the natural facts of linguistic geography. Jacob Grimm
appeals to the law that "it is not rivers or mountains that form
the womb of a people; rather, their language alone establishes
the borders of a people, dispersed over mountain and
stream."[14] This conviction, moreover, constitutes the background for the ambitions of the jurists and historians who
devoted the first public session of the Germanists' assembly to
denouncing the Danish crown's claim to Schleswig, which was
not even a member of the German federation.

In 1874, Wilhelm Scherer characterized the spirit of the Historical School, in retrospect, with a series of conceptual pairs:

> Nationality against cosmopolitanism; the force of nature against
> artificial cultivation; autonomous powers against centralization;
> self-governance against satisfaction from above; individual free-
> dom against the omnipotence of the state; the dignity of history
> against the constructed ideal; the honoring of the ancient against
> the hunt for the new; development against artificial fabrication;
> feeling and intuition against understanding and logic; organic
> against mathematical form; the sensuous against the abstract;
> natural creative powers against the rule; the living against the
> mechanistic.[15]

We can immediately recognize here how the ideology of the
"spirit of the people" converges with the liberal goals of the
nationalist movement. In the spontaneous growth of the spirit
of the people, described with such reverence, we can also read
the productive, regenerative, indeed the emancipatory power
that stood opposed to the regimentation of a frozen state
bureaucracy and demanded that "the people" assume a political form befitting its historical nature. On the other hand,
Scherer's description also conveys the antiquarian, backward-
looking, quietistic, and anti-enlightenment features that did not
exactly predestine historicism for a role as midwife to the birth
of a modern, civil nation-state.

To be sure, the philosophical idealism of the Tübingen writers displayed a dynamic similar to that of the romantic-historical thought of Herder, Möser, and Hamann. Hölderlin, Schelling, and Hegel also invoked the power of the imagination, productivity, and sensuous spontaneity against the classifications of the understanding and the positivities of a frozen tradition. They too emphasized the stubborn individuality of the particular within the structure of an organic whole as opposed to the abstract and the general. But philosophy appropriated this very opposition as the problem of a contradictory moment of reason itself; whereas for historicism, concepts for the rational and the general remained lacking. Without such a relation to reason, the Germanists had to struggle with the problem of how the fundamental principles of a liberal constitution could be spun out of the "spirit of the people."

III.   The Dialectic of Inclusion and Exclusion

The worldview of the humanities thus saw the political unification of Germany as the long-overdue realization of a national unity that had already developed on the level of culture. All that was missing from the body politic, itself defined through culture and language, was the appropriate political clothing. The linguistic community had to coincide with the legal community within one nation-state. Each nation, it seemed, possessed a claim to political independence as its birthright. But in choosing to interpret this principle through the doctrine of the spirit of a people, the participants in the Germanists' assembly deceived themselves about the specifically modern aspect of their own program. Because they assumed that the nation-state had already developed into maturity along with the cultural nation, they failed to recognize the constructive character of their own project. The spirit of the German people – which was supposed to assume a concrete political form in a new political order – had in fact already been documented in the most ancient sources of German poetry, language, and law. This contradiction helps to explain the cognitive dissonances that

emerged in the course of the debate on national unification. It is
the very assumption of a homogenous, clearly delimited linguistic community that sets a peculiar dialectic in motion.

Even in the case of a Greater German solution to the problem of national unity, the cultural borders of the linguistic
community could not be adequately reconciled with the political borders of a legal community. In each case, the borders of
the nation-state would both exclude German-speaking minorities and include non-German-speaking ones. The political-legal
exclusion of Germans living abroad generated the desire for
their cultural-linguistic incorporation. Hence the historians
proposed the foundation of a "Union for the Preservation of
German Nationality Abroad." The proposal aimed at two
objectives: for many of the speakers, the fate of emigrants
(many of whom were streaming into North America in unprecedented numbers at mid-century) lay close to the heart; the
Union would help emigrants "preserve their customary and
original language, and therewith also warm relations to the
Motherland(!)"[16] But such a policy required other "means
and ends" for "Europe, or, better, Germany's bordering states"
than "for foreign parts of the world."[17] Without wishing an
"intervention into the realm of the political," Georg Heinrich
Perz, reporting for the historians, reminded the assembly of the
"Germans in Alsace, in Lorraine, in the Netherlands, the Germans living beyond the Niemen, the Germans of Bohemia, of
Hungary and Transylvania, who have a right to the continued
preservation of their German nationality and their mother
tongue."[18] In his opening address, Jacob Grimm had already
commented on the regrettable "special path" of the Dutch
language, "this particular, weakened form of the language to
our northwest," observing that "as it hardly seems possible that
we will be able to bring it back to us, it becomes all the more
desirable to multiply the contacts between it and our own
language."[19]

The split between High and Low German is a reminder of the
price that the imaginary unity of the linguistic nation demands
– the standardization of dialect forms, which Grimm describes
euphemistically in the terms of profit and loss.[20] His brother
Wilhelm concedes the artificial character of written language,

without which the "tribes will often not understand one another at all." There is nothing originary about the homogeneity of the linguistic community; it requires a leveling of different dialects in favor of a written language imposed by administrative means. But the fact that all those valuable national particularities could only be manufactured through the active repression of already developed particularities fits rather poorly with the antiquarian conception of the organic spirit of the people. No less bothersome is the fact that the very national languages that supposedly ground the individuality of different peoples are themselves the products of long processes of mutual interaction and influence, making any such clearly demarcated linguistic unities impossible.

In comparison with "mixed" languages such as English or even French, German was of course still regarded at this time as a "pure" language. But German too was replete with borrowed words of forgotten Latin origins, foreign terms that were used even in everyday language, and numerous terminological expressions that were indispensable for specialized fields of knowledge. Wilhelm Grimm mentions these facts without "advocating any foreign intrusion." He holds out the hope that his *Dictionary* will "reawaken the purity of language." His purism was, perhaps, not of that harsh or "straightlaced" kind that he himself had always fought against. But it is ominous enough that he, like his brother,[21] also struggled against the corruption of the familiar by the foreign:

> All the gates are thrown open for herding in foreign creations. The kernels of our noble language lie mixed among the chaff; who has the shovel to scatter them over the threshing floor! How often have I seen the well-favored face, nay, the spiritually rich features of these sheaves deformed. The first book one opens – I do not even say a bad book – out swarm the countless vermin before our eyes.[22]

In this respect things were even more difficult for the German jurists than for the philologists. While foreign languages formed nothing more than a background for the philologists, Roman law still ruled in the jurists' own country: "Our law

contradicts the life, the popular consciousness, the needs, customs, opinions, and attitudes of the people.[23] With Beseler,
Mittermaier, and Reyscher, the Germanists' assembly could
count the leading figures of "modern" German jurisprudence
as its members. Like the older Historical Legal School, these
thinkers all opposed rational law, instead cultivating legal history as "the only path to a true perception of our own condition" (Savigny). But unlike Savigny, they emphasized the
contradiction between the "law of the people" and the "law
of the jurists."[24] They were convinced that law, as the expression of the spirit of the people, must assume a different form
in each nation; the acceptance of foreign law would *per
se* destroy a legal culture rooted in the ethical life of a people.[25]
This juristic version of the doctrine of the spirit of a people
runs into three major difficulties: (a) the jurists had a good
deal of trouble accounting for the superiority of doctrinal
Roman law; (b) it must have appeared paradoxical to them
that several institutions of received Germanic law were able
to establish themselves against Roman law only on the basis of
specifically modern economic conditions; and (c) above all,
they were unable to provide the bases of legitimation for a
democratic constitutional state from their own legal-historical
resources.

(a) The products of particularistic local, regional, and urban
legal codes remained so far below the level of fully developed
Roman law that the jurists simply had no choice but to
acknowledge the superiority of Roman law, above all in the
areas of civil law. Some of the speakers attempted to downplay
this fact by claiming that Roman law had been considerably
modified, even "Germanized," through the practice of common law and the long exposure to "Germanic customs, attitudes, and political and social conditions."[26] Others, however,
warned against regarding Germanic and Roman law as sworn
enemies: "We can only return to a state of barbarism if we wish
to root out all that Roman law has given us."[27] One speaker
distinguished the scientific or formal side of Roman law from its
contents: "That which is good and useful, which has developed
in scholarly circles in all civilized states, we wish to adopt,

insofar as it corresponds with our purposes; and this is itself a demand of civilization that is not opposed to nationality, which should not allow itself to drift into formal isolation."[28]

(b) But it is not just purism that leads the jurists into difficulties. Their attitude toward legal antiquities that are unsuited to the conditions of modern life is also problematic. Mittermaier's examples of the superiority of Germanic law over the Justinianic code unintentionally reveal the irony of these attempts to reach back to ancient traditions. German legal institutions could only make progress into peripheral areas such as commercial law, securities, and corporate law because specific elements of medieval urban laws had proven themselves to be functional within modern commercial economies. It was only on this basis that the juridical section of the Germanists' assembly could see their task of "excluding foreign elements" as the attempt "to determine those legal institutions that have arisen on German soil through modern commerical conditions."[29]

(c) For liberal legal historians, however, the real challenge lay not in private but in public law, where the competition was not so much one between Germanic and Roman law but between historical and natural law. There was obviously no home-grown equivalent for the grounding of the modern constitutional order in natural law. And yet the unified nation required a constitution modelled on the revolutionary constitutions of America and France. There was certainly agreement on the need for a "general legislation": since Savigny, the German jurists had regarded themselves as an unpolitical substitute for a legislative branch. But they had in mind primarily the codification of civil law, like the later Code of Civil Law, whereby the parliament only had the authority to ratify substantial legal contents that were already rooted in the ethical life and habits of the people.[30] As long as law is able to generate its own legitimacy from the legally formative power of the people, no need arises for a legitimation of positive law which would have to be met by the democratic procedures of a parliamentary legislature. The liberal legal historians do draw a historical line from the Germanic *thing*-meetings, rural village assemblies, lay courts, and estates to modern forms of popular representation. But their calls for freedom of the press and other basic legal rights – the schedule of rights that would be exhaustively enumerated in paragraphs 131 through 189 of the *Paulskirche* constitution two short years later – could not be supported from the sources of German law. In the end, even Reycher could only hope "that reason would of itself lead to a certain agreement on legal concepts."[31]

We see once again how poorly the idea of an originary, homogenous and clearly defined "nation of the people" conforms with the universalistic heritage of political liberalism. A Professor Gaup, from Breslau, takes a step still further back: referring to an *original* mixing of the Germanic and Roman peoples, he introduces a non-identitarian reading of the doctrine of the spirit of the people, pleading for the "development of noble humanity on the basis of deeply felt nationality." He recalls Goethe's idea of a world literature, identifying it with a spirit "which we ourselves call the occidental, a spirit that dominates in America just the same as in Europe."[32] Georg Gottfried Gervinus had already produced his five-volume *History of the Poetical National Literature of the Germans* (Leipzig, 1835–42) from this same perspective.

IV. From the Spirit of the People to the Nation of Citizens

Next to Dahlman, Gervinus was the most prominent of the historians at the Frankfurt Germanists' assembly. He had occasionally warned his countrymen against "national vanity and boastfulness,"[33] and regarded Germany's classical period, from Lessing to Goethe, as an aesthetic resource for the political emancipation of the German nation.[34] Unlike most of his colleagues, Gervinus was not discouraged by the failed revolution of 1848. In 1852, the publication of the widely read *Introduction* to his history of the nineteenth century plunged him into a notorious trial for high treason.[35] The text describes his "standpoint on the political development in the recent historical epoch," and presents a panorama of struggle for the ideals of freedom and democracy, a struggle that draws its energy from a tense interplay between the Germanic and Roman spirits from the late Middle Ages through the Reformation and the American and French revolutions, to the liberation movements of the nineteenth century. The political movements of the present were "borne by the instincts of the masses" and tended "toward internal freedom or toward external independence, and mostly toward both at once."[36] To be sure, Gervinus also criticized those abstract, cosmopolitan ideals "that seek to wipe away the differences amongst peoples," and described what he called the "double-sided" aspect of popular political movements: they struggle "internally toward freer civil orders; externally toward safeguarding the independence of peoples and nations, toward a political order that reflects the natural separation of nationalities and languages."[37] Nevertheless, all people struggle for the same political goals, and this fact sets in motion an interaction between the spirits of different peoples, who can communicate with and learn from one another.

Gervinus was an enthusiastic reader of de Tocqueville, and saw the democratic constitution of America as "the model and the preference of the masses." The new civil ideal of the United States, superseding the models of classical antiquity, was no longer based on legal archaisms but on modern conditions that generate both egalitarianism and individualism at once.

> The desire for equality in all relationships, the freedom of one person toward another, is necessarily rooted in the self-regard of personality. But political equality, if it is not to be merely a different expression of despotic oppression, demands the will of the people for the decision of the majority, and establishes a government no longer grounded in the false pretenses of divine law . . . ; it demands a legislation that arises from the needs of society, needs which are determined by the collective itself.[38]

Legal principles such as these no longer contradict national particularity. They arise from a peculiar interplay of differing spirits of peoples.

The ideals of religious and political freedom that had first arisen in the Protestant-Germanic countries were disseminated throughout Europe and then to America, and only then began their long return trip eastward. But these ideals only returned to Europe after being filtered through the multiconfessional and multicultural milieu of American society, and were thus purified of religious and nationalistic "additives." This, in any case, is how Gervinus describes the influence of the American Revolution on the Revolution in France:

> As American freedoms migrate to France, they prove their universal character... The political ideal had freed itself from its religious supplements in America; indeed, under American democracy, in which all members live in equal satisfaction, it had freed itself even from national limitations. The Protestant-Germanic particularism was no longer a condition for its continued influence. With this reorientation, it mastered the greatest of the Catholic and Romanic peoples. And thus it opened an entirely new world.[39]

The mission was clear, and the audience understood it only too well: the "triumphal march of freedom" that had begun in France now waited impatiently to complete itself in the country where the Protestant idea of freedom had first been born.

In this manner, Gervinus succeeded in grafting the universal form of the democratic constitutional state onto the particularistic doctrine of the "spirit of the people." The Germanic and the Roman gradually loosen themselves from their rootedness in concrete peoples, and are transformed into principles extending from one country to another. Under Gervinus' historical gaze, the people and "the spirit of the people" lose their clear linguistic outline. Gervinus thus has no clear answer to the question "what is a people?" He could have got one from Julius Fröbel, the Southwest German democrat and politically active nephew of the educational reformer, who like Gervinus was fascinated by "democracy in America," and later sat with Gervinus as a delegate in the National Assembly at the *Paulskirche*.

At the time of the Frankfurt Germanists' assembly, Fröbel published (under the pseudonym C. Junius) a work that can be

read as an advance commentary on Jacob Grimm's definition of
a people: a people, Fröbel writes, is

> the totality of all persons who speak the same language; (but)
> they actually may own this language as a fundamental part of an
> ancestral community; or they may be the product of a mixture
> of different ancestries, producing a new people; or they may also
> be a people who have utterly abandoned their language and have
> merged into another people...A people may, further, be the
> totality of persons speaking a common language who go on to
> form a single state, a number of states, or a federation of states;
> or a people may be a component of different states; finally, a
> people may live dispersed, with no homeland and entirely with-
> out a political existence.[40]

For descriptive purposes, neither a purely political nor a purely
genealogical concept of a people is adequate, since peoples arise
and vanish "in the course of culture." Looked at normatively, it
is only a people's desire for democratic self-determination that
can legitimate the demand for political independence: "The
ethical, free, political moment in the existence of a people is
freely chosen fellowship."[41] Republican freedom thus takes
normative priority over the freedom of the nation.[42] Fröbel,
who had lived in Switzerland, clearly recognized the importance of prepolitical – even if only imagined – commonalities of
a shared cultural form of life for a collective republican existence: "A common language and literature, a collective mode of
art and ethics" is a precious good, a resource of social solidarity
for a people who "maintain their existence chiefly through free
associations and voluntary fellowships." As we ourselves now
approach the threshold of a postnational form of collective
political life, we may still be able to learn something from
Fröbel's clear-eyed reflections.

The Maastricht Treaty establishes a basis for the development of the European Union beyond the status of a functional
economic community. But in a politically united Europe, policy
decisions cutting across different political spheres, including
social policy, would be equally binding for all member states –
for Danes and Spaniards in just the same way as for Greeks and
Germans. Accepting decisions whose consequences have to be

borne equally by all requires a form of abstract solidarity that was first produced during the nineteenth century between citizens of different nation-states. The Danes must learn to see a Spaniard, the Germans a Greek, as "one of us," just as, conversely, the Spaniards a Dane and the Greeks a German. There is no form of collective political life in which the necessary equalization of different interest positions and living conditions could arise solely from the cool calculation of individual advantage. This is why political scientists search for "non-majoritarian sources of legitimacy" for the Europe of the future. A consciousness of collective belonging is necessary if "freely associated allies" are to identify with one another as citizens.

In the nineteenth century, the peoples of Europe – each on its own, of course – were faced with a structurally similar problem. A European identity, which today has to be created from a communicative context stretching over national public spheres, was at that time the product of national elites, and took the form of a double-sided national consciousness. Of course, the idea of the nation in its populist version led to devastating acts of exclusion, to the expulsion of enemies of the state – and to the annihilation of Jews. But in its culturalistic version, the idea of the nation also contributed to the creation of a mode of solidarity between persons who had until then remained strangers to one another. The universalistic reformulation of inherited loyalties to village and clan, landscape and dynasty was a difficult and protracted process, and it did not permeate the entire population until well into the twentieth century, even in the classical nation-states of the West. Regarding the political unification of Europe, we now stand, if not in an entirely comparable situation, then certainly before a similar task to the one that our Germanists faced for the political unification of their nation.

By expanding the parameters for the implementation of human rights and democracy, the nation-state made possible a new, more abstract form of social integration beyond the borders of ancestry and dialect. Today we are faced with the task of carrying on this process with a further abstractive step. A process of democratic will-formation that can cross national borders needs a unified context, and this in turn requires the development of a European public sphere and a common European political culture. In a postnational communicative context of this sort, an awareness of collective membership needs to emerge from the background of an already existing fabric of interests. Perhaps we can take some encouragement from an insight that our colleagues in the *Vormärz* didn't have: collective identities are made, not found. But they can only unify the heterogenous. Citizens who share a common political life also are others to one another, and each is entitled to *remain* an Other.

V. The Unpolitical Self-Understanding of German Philology

In light of this current challenge, the Frankfurt Germanists' assembly understandably confronts us with the question of why, ever since that first, failed attempt, German universities have never again undertaken any comparable initiative to exert an influence on the political public sphere. In my conclusion I will use the example of German philology to describe a tendency internal to the development of the discipline itself. From a sociological perspective, academic disciplines such as German studies assume an array of different functions. Along with the goals of research and professional training, they also serve the goal of general education and the public process of reaching understanding.[43] German philology fulfilled these functions in a notably asymmetrical way: it remained fundamentally preoccupied with scholarly research. But this unreflective devotion to scholarship did not protect the discipline from a false politicization.

At a distance, the history of German philology appears to conform to a developmental pattern that sociologists of science have proposed for academic disciplines in general. Around 1800, the medieval scholarly societies in Germany were restructured into a state-supported university system with both research and pedagogical functions. The *Universitas* of scholarly disciplines replaced the medieval hierarchy of higher and lower faculties, and these disciplines, embodied in disciplinary communities, differentiated themselves from one another horizontally. This differentiation also produced a new form of scholarship. Scholarly work was transformed from the systematic enumeration of received knowledge to the methodical manufacture of new knowledge, on the model of modern research in the natural sciences. The singular term "science" no longer described the virtue of scholarliness that an individual might exhibit, but rather referred to the rationality of an impersonal procedure that one followed.

As is often remarked, Lachmann's appeal of 1818 and Jacob Grimm's *Deutsche Grammatik* of 1819 mark the date of German scholarship's decisive break from the dilettantish approach to German literature – not just from the antiquarian work of scholars of the older sort, but also from the work of amateurs and from a patriotic enthusiasm for old German texts that was nourished by the anti-French sentiments of the time.[44] Once the discipline had developed a philological identity, the institutionalization of professorships, disciplinary societies, and scholarly communication quickly followed. Along with Romance and Slavic philology, German philology made up the disciplinary canon for modern philologists. It established itself as a subject of secondary education and delivered up literary histories to a middle-class public intent on self-cultivation. Finally, the discipline differentiated itself internally between ancient and modern German philology; historical linguistics separated off from general linguistics. As a plurality of research programs and methodologies emerged over the course of the twentieth century, German philology appeared to have completed the normal career path of a scholarly discipline.

On closer inspection, however, this historical profile of the discipline exhibits a number of peculiarities. One might have supposed that the discipline would have had any number of possible political entanglements; indeed it would be surprising if a discipline that specialized in a national literature and a nation's mother tongue didn't have a greater proximity to social and cultural life, and hence to the political public sphere, than other disciplines. But astonishingly, university linguistics remained entirely fixated on its scholarly mission: during the

entire nineteenth century it steadfastly shielded itself from all
social imperatives. Its relations to educational and professional
development, as well as to the reading public and the political
public sphere, remained underdeveloped in relation to its
predominating research orientation. German philology only
inadequately fulfilled its tasks of professional preparation, general education, and participation in processes of public understanding.

It is because German philology gained a disciplinary identity
primarily in the work of text-immanent criticism that Karl
Lachmann, with a background in classical philology, could
play such a dominant role in the early years of the discipline.
German philology could offer proof of its own scholarly rigor
with methods borrowed from classical philology. This was
undoubtedly important for the constitution of the discipline.
But after this early phase had ended, the adoption of the same
methodological consciousness of other, long-established disciplines obviously contributed to the fetishization of German philology's claim to scholarly status; a claim that professors who
had little interest in education, public influence, or populariza-
tion found it easy to hide behind. In its aloofness, the discipline
only grudgingly acceded to demands that it open itself up to
secondary schools and the public. The so-called Nibelung controversy, ignited by Lachmann's own ascetic editorial practice,
can also be understood as a product of this particular motivation. The opposing parties accused one another of pointless
overspecialization, on the one side, and well-meaning dilettant-
ism on the other.[45]

"Philologization" also meant the end of the sweeping, expa-
tiatory form of literary history in the style of Gervinus and
Prutz, which was meant to serve the enlightenment of the
general public. That form of literary history came to be
regarded as journalistic and unscholarly, and fell out of favor
after 1848. Klaus Weimar writes of the "expulsion of spirit
from literary history," which from then on would be tailored
to fit the format of a historical-philological research program.
Beginning in the middle of the nineteenth century, literary
histories were removed from the jurisdiction of philosophers
and historians and placed into the hands of German philolo-

gists, who had acquired their disciplinary reputations in the field of old German philology. They had been trained to edit and comment on texts, to provide explanations of words and word usages, but not to interpret texts.[46] Wilhelm Scherer's *History of German Literature* (I have an inherited copy of the 1910 12th edition from my father's student years) is an obvious exception to this.

In general, university-based German philologists closed themselves off both to the needs of the broader public and to the secondary schools. Until the end of the nineteenth century, philological instruction in the German *Gymnasia* remained instruction in ancient languages and classical literatures. Latin and Greek still maintained an educational monopoly; German played only a marginal role in the daily curriculum.[47] The problem was not that the lobbying efforts of the Prussian cultural ministry were too weak. After analyzing the protocols of the "Assembly of German Philologists and Schoolmasters" between 1862 and 1934, Detlev Kopp reached the conclusion that the German philologists were simply uninterested in assuming a larger share of responsibility for instruction: "The chief interest of university-based German studies consisted in the goal of raising the status of the discipline in the academic hierarchy, far more than extending its practice into the secondary schools."[48]

If German philology, in its desire to base its entire reputation on scholarly research, only grudgingly and inadequately took on its social and cultural tasks, this fact still says nothing about the discipline's latent influence on the mentality of the cultured middle classes. Early German philology, as we have seen, was rooted in a philosophy of the humanities that honored linguistic monuments and literary inheritances as documents of the "spirit of the people." Against this background, the strict methodological treatment of texts takes on ritualistic features: textual analysis comes to be regarded as the reverent, identity-granting reappropriation of an infinitely valuable cultural store. Selected texts are elevated into a literary canon. The esoteric discipline's professional ethos – securing, protecting, and purifying texts that belong to the national heritage – had a broad effect on the processes of consciousness-formation: it established the canon of definitive national cultural goods. German philology,

> which in a first step employed the methods of ancient philology for medieval texts in vernacular languages, and then in a second step turned to German literary history... finds its complement in the canonization of the authors of German classicism. What the historical sciences had set into motion was, with the canonization of the classics, lifted out of the course of time and frozen in place for quiet contemplation or compulsory appreciation.[49]

Humanism had at its disposal the concept of "the classical" to describe the intrinsic worth of those objects that served as sites for the self-realization of Spirit. As early as the work of Friedrich Schlegel, however, the concept of the classical had been freed from its reference to classical antiquity and became available for other uses: it could be applied to modern objects as well.[50] Modern philologists, particularly German philologists, reaped the benefits of this change. The reader could now consider as "classical" any work from which one could learn something essential, no matter how small or great the temporal distance between work and reader might be.[51] The question is: who decides what is essential? Neither text nor reader can independently determine the essential content of a text; its status as a classic must be demonstrated in the act of reading itself. The indeterminacy resulting from this was one that German philology could quite easily resolve, since philological method (which first makes the text accessible to the reader) is bound up with the authorizing force of the spirit of the people. This authority grounds, *per se*, the supposition that all those texts that express the "spirit of the people" have an identity-forming, i.e. an essential, content. The relation to the authentic spirit of the people which Herder had claimed for the early humanities charged German philology with a cultural mission that it believed only a philological discipline could fulfill. As a science, then, it used its editorial practices to help shift a pietistically overburdened idea of cultivation from "humanity" to "the nation."

At least since imperial Germany, the unpolitical ethos of scholarly rigor went hand in hand with a mentality shaped by national myths – not least in the minds of the German philologists themselves.

This reflects what Aleida Assmann has called the "coevolution of scientization and secularization." A social division of labor developed: on the one side, differentiated scholarly disciplines that oversee and canonize the national heritage; on the other side, an undifferentiated notion of cultivation or *Bildung* raised to cultic status, whose (only apparently private) function was the production of vapidly nationalistic attitudes. In the schools, which the university-based German philologists had left to their own devices, German instruction took on the character of a consecrated ceremony. The classic German writers were celebrated as heroes of Spirit; their works were worshiped but never analyzed.[52] A literary culture based on clubs and monuments, commemorative readings, literary pilgrimages, and memorial celebrations, attests to how a literature processed by a nationalist pedagogy is celebrated in the political public sphere: "The religious content of the ideal of *Bildung* gains its clearest profile at the point where the tendentiously irresistible developmental course of scholarship collides with objects that have been reinforced into absolute values."[53]

Of course, German philology had to pay a high price for its own sterility. In the period before the First World War, figures outside the discipline such as Wilhelm Dilthey or Georg Simmel took over the interpretation of literary works. In 1911, Friedrich Gundolf's *Shakespeare and the German Spirit* had an enormous impact. Moreover, the discipline itself took an "intellectual-historical turn," largely in response to Dilthey's collection of essays, *Experience and Poetry* (1906). With this turn, university-based scholarship finally opened itself to the secondary schools and the reading public.[54] But the cult of Poetry simply became the domain of a methodologically weakened discipline, which was all the easier to politicize from within. The orientation toward intellectual and historical backgrounds and contexts certainly cleared the way for a hermeneutical approach to artworks, but it also blocked other paths that might have loosened the fixation on the familiar, the trusted, and the honored. Efforts to develop a comparative literary history, as the Romance languages had done, foundered; the new sociology of literature, which illuminated the social-functional contexts of literary production and reception, was thoroughly marginalized; an aesthetic theory that might have pointed out the radical alterities and dissonances in the conceptual beginnings of modernism never got off the ground, despite Worringer.[55]

In 1932, Leo Löwenthal was forced to defend a rational, analytical attitude toward literary objects against the poverty of a "closed, irrationalistic front of literary science" preoccupied with the "secrets of the poetic soul."[56] Löwenthal's essay, "On the Social Situation of Literature", appeared in the first volume of the *Zeitschrift für Sozialforschung*, which was also the last volume to appear in Germany. Together with a triumphalist intellectual history, a very different spirit had overtaken the German universities. Theodor W. Adorno, even more than Benjamin, forms the quintessential countertype to this spirit. Adorno brought together Eichendorff and Surrealism;[57] the inwardness of aesthetic structure and the exteriority of social praxis.[58] After his return from exile, he directed those long-repressed research alternatives against a mode of thinking that was oriented exclusively by intellectual history, bringing them into prominence even within the discipline of German philology – as is exemplified by the work of Peter Szondi.

2

On the Public Use of
History

The Democracy Prize, last awarded in 1990 to Bärbel Bohley
and Wolfgang Ullman on behalf of the civil rights activists of
the GDR, is given to this year's recipient on the following
grounds: through the "urgency, the forcefulness, and the
moral strength of his presentation" Daniel Goldhagen has
"provided a powerful stimulus to the public conscience of the
Federal Republic"; he has sharpened "our sensibility for what
constitutes the background and the limit of a German 'normalization.'" This reference to the rhetorical effect of the book,
and to the controversial issue of normalization (which poses
itself anew in the transition to a Berlin Republic) makes clear
what the Board of Trustees of the *Blätter für deutsche und
internationale Politik* has in mind in awarding this prize – and
what it does not. It cannot and will not enter into a controversy
amongst professional historians. In Germany as well as in the
United States, a number of prominent historians have made
great contributions, even devoted entire careers, to the research
of the Nazi period and the political enlightenment of German
citizens concerning the complex prehistory of the Holocaust.
Here I will name only Martin Broszat, Hans Mommsen, and
Eberhard Jaeckel, and younger historians such as Ulrich
Herbert, Dietrich Pohl, and Thomas Sandkühler, as representative. The question is not which contemporary historians
would have deserved the attention of a wider public, but rather
how we are to understand the unusual degree of public attention that Daniel Goldhagen's book has in fact received. Awarding this prize communicates the conviction that the public

response that both the book and its author have found in the Federal Republic is as deserved as it is welcome.[1]

This view has been the subject of vehement dispute. Its critics charge the book with offering a global, one-dimensional presentation of a highly complex event, and thus of satisfying the mass public's demand for oversimplified explanations. They object that the book employs an aesthetics of the gruesome as a stylistic tool, generating emotional effects that dim the capacity for sober judgment. Other criticisms refer less to the text itself and far more to the motives of those who buy and read it. Here we encounter the familiar stereotypes: "do-goodism," "negative nationalism", "flight from history." With a retrospective identification with the victims, so it is said, the descendants of the perpetrators have provided themselves with a cost-free, self-justifying satisfaction: grabbing once again at a chance to renounce their loyalty to their own traditions and fleeing into the chimerical realm of the postnational. I must confess that I do not entirely understand these agitated reactions. They are trying to explain a phenomenon that stands in no need of explanation.

Clearly, a broad public response to a book such as this cannot come as a great surprise: one need only see how Goldhagen's analytical case histories of the annihilation of the Jews mesh with the expectations of a reading public as it searches for an understanding of this criminal chapter of its own history. Goldhagen's investigations are tailored to address precisely those questions that have polarized our public and private discussions for the past half-century. From the very beginnings of the Federal Republic, there has been a fundamental disagreement between all those who would prefer to interpret the breakdown of civilization as if it were a natural event, on the one side, and those on the other side who insist on seeing it as the consequence of the actions of responsible persons – and not just of Hitler and his inner circle. Today, both sides square off with mutual suspicions of each others' respective motives: the diagnosis of denial thus stands opposed to the accusation of self-righteous moralizing. This hopeless battle only serves to conceal the truly fundamental question at issue: what is the meaning of a retrospective ascription of criminal responsibility, which we undertake in the present for the ends of the ethical-political process of understanding among citizens? Goldhagen provides a new stimulus for a reflection on the proper public use of history.

In public discourses of self-understanding, which can be touched off by films, television series, or exhibitions just as much as by historical works or "affairs," we argue not so much over short-terms goals and policies as over the forms of a desired political existence, and over the values that shall predominate in it. Moreover, such discourses concern how we as citizens of the Federal Republic can mutually respect one another, and how we wish to be recognized by others. National history constitutes an important background for this. National traditions and mentalities reach back far behind the origins of this Republic, forming a part of our personal identities. This connection between political self-understanding and historical awareness also determines the way that Goldhagen's book is relevant for us. A singular crime – a crime that first gave rise to the notion of a "crime against humanity" – issued from the very midst of our collective life. For this reason, all those members of later generations who struggle to come to terms with their political existence in this country are faced with the same question: can the responsibility for mass political criminality ever be laid as a burden on individual persons or groups of persons? If so, who were the responsible actors, and what were their reasons for acting as they did? And were normative justifications, insofar as they were of decisive importance for the actors, rooted in the culture and forms of thought?

Goldhagen ascribes to a representative group of committed perpetrators a subjective justification for their actions that itself formed an integral part of the basic cultural convictions dominant at the time: "The rupture in the German cultural fabric that the Jews represented to Germans . . . was such that cultural taboos failed to hold sway when the Germans discussed the Jews."[2] This cannot but have a powerful impact on our own self-understanding. In their forms of thinking and feeling, their gestures and expressions, and in their ways of seeing, past and present generations are woven together in a tapestry composed of countless cultural threads. To the extent to which it is legitimate, an assertion such as this must shake any naive trust in our own traditions. This critical attitude toward one's own particularity is precisely what Goldhagen's study demands – and what worries some conservatives.

These conservative circles believe that only unquestioned traditions and strong values make a people "able for the future." Hence each and every skeptical look back at tradition is suspected as yet another instance of unbridled moralizing. Since 1989, a new sort of patriotic spirit has gained strength in the unified Germany, according to which the learning processes of the last forty years have already gone "too far." In a journal entry from June 19, 1948, Carl Schmitt dismissed a "repentance preacher" like Karl Jaspers as beneath attention. The wretched vocabulary of repression audible in his dreadful *Glossarium*, raging against a "false eagerness to repent" at every attempt at self criticism, was reconstituted in Weikersheim; in the wake of successful diversionary tactics against "political correctness," it still exerts an influence well beyond the inner circle of the truly incorrigible. Even those who think differently than these hard-core conservatives seem to worry that Goldhagen's study will provoke a questionable moral judgment of the unwitting contemporaries of the Holocaust. And yet this study can serve as an illustration of how the historical problem of subjective accountability bears an entirely distinct status once it enters the contemporary context of an ethical-political process of self-understanding. I will first recall the general sense in which a public use of history can be legitimate, and then go on to explain why Goldhagen's case histories are well-suited for an ethical-political process of self-understanding free from moralistic misapprehensions.

I

Modern historiography is addressed to two different audiences: the guild of professional historians and the general reading public. A good work of contemporary history should simultaneously satisfy both the critical standards of the profession, and

the expectations of an interested public. Of course the view of
the historian must not be directed by the interests of readers,
who come to the historical text searching for explanations of
their own historical situation. The moment that the analytic
perspective of the observer mingles with the perspective
assumed by participants in a discourse of collective self-understanding, historiographical science degenerates into the politics
of history. The union of historicism and nationalism once arose
from just this confusion; a similar confusion is reflected today in
attempts to continue the Cold War by historiographic means. It
goes without saying that only historians of integrity, who insist
upon the difference between observer and participant perspectives, are capable of being reliable experts.

Political criminal justice, for example, depends on historical
expertise. In cases of mass political criminality, both jurisprudence and contemporary history deal with the same questions
of accountability. Both take an interest in who participated in
crimes; whether responsibility for the consequences of criminal
actions should be borne by persons or ascribed to circumstances; whether those involved could have acted differently;
whether in a given case they acted on the basis of normative
convictions or out of self-interest; whether another choice of
behavior could reasonably have been expected of them, and so
forth. But the criminal judge can only make good use of historical documentation – just as, conversely, the historian can only
profitably use the official proceedings of the office of the public
prosecutor – as long as both, judge and historian, view the same
phenomenon from different perspectives. The one side is interested in the question of the culpability for an act; the other in
the explanation of its cause. From the historian's perspective,
accountability for actions is not resolved in terms of guilt or
innocence, but in terms of what kind of explanatory grounds
exist. However that explanation will look – whether the causes
lie predominantly in persons or in circumstances – a causal
explanation can neither condemn nor excuse the actors. Only
from the perspective of participants who encounter one
another and call each other to account for their actions,
whether in a court of law or on the street, do questions of
accountability change into legal – or moral – questions.

The moral point of view also concerns the judgment of justice or injustice, although of course without the strict procedural rules of a criminal court. Naturally, everyday forms of historical knowledge can be employed for moral controversies just as for the ends of criminal justice – as in the proverbial struggle between "fathers and sons." In both cases, historical knowledge becomes relevant in the same way for those affected. However, the moral point of view, the view toward justice, differs sharply from the point of view of members of a current generation as they seek to reassure themselves about a historical heritage which they, as citizens and members of a collective political life, must inherit in one way or another.

It is this difference that concerns me. From the point of view of the *ethical-political* processes of self-understanding of citizens, the explanatory accounts of the historian have a different function than they would have in moral or legal discourses.

Here, in an ethical-political discourse, the question is not primarily the guilt or innocence of the forefathers but rather the critical self-assurance of their descendants. The public interest of those born later, who cannot know how they themselves would have acted in the same situation, has a different goal than the zeal of morally judgmental contemporaries of the Nazi years, who find themselves in the same context of interaction and demand a moral reckoning from each other. Painful revelations of the conduct of one's own parents and grandparents can only be an occasion for sorrow; they remain a private affair between those intimately involved. On the other hand, as citizens, members of subsequent generations take a public interest in the darkest chapter of their national history with regard to themselves. They are not pointing a finger of blame at anyone else. They are trying to bring about some clarity concerning the cultural matrix of a burdened inheritance, to recognize what they themselves are collectively liable for, and what is to be continued, and what revised, of those traditions that once had formed such a disastrous motivational background. An awareness of collective liability emerges from the widespread guilty conduct of individuals in the past. This has nothing to do with the ascription of collective guilt, a notion that is simply incoherent on conceptual grounds alone.[3]

II

Within a specific theoretical framework, Goldhagen's case histories, particularly his studies of police battalions and death marches, use observed modes of behavior to draw conclusions about orientational interpretive patterns and mentalities. The social-scientific studies read like retrospectively conducted experiments, and in this sense assume the character of independent research. At the same time, however, the analytical perspectives encompassing the responsible perpetrators, the motivational grounds for their extraordinary actions, and the fundamental cognitive patterns that generated them, accommodate the public's interest in a forthright, non-moralizing self-understanding that we, in the country of the perpetrators, surely have. Of course, a clear analytical strategy cannot in itself decide the correctness of its results. But in the meantime, a number of professional controversies over the details of Goldhagen's work have been helpful in de-dramatizing its reception. Specialists familiar with the historical material have raised a host of objections concerning specific details, while taking Goldhagen's overall approach seriously.[4]

I myself am won over by the clear argumentative strategy. Goldhagen defines the circle of perpetrators he is investigating as constituted by membership in the institutions of murder, and by direct participation in the operations of killing Jews. These perpetrators may be said to stand at the end of a complex chain of events. Defining the perpetrators in this way implicitly resolves questions of objective accountability, which are far from easy to decide in light of the highly anonymous, differentiated, and administrative execution of organized mass murder. At the same time, other questions – which norms were violated, and whether the perpetrators had knowledge of them – are settled by simple reference to the form of the crime itself. The analysis proper then begins with the question of whether the perpetrators acted in a subjectively accountable manner, whether they were aware of, and desired, the foreseeable and avoidable consequences of their actions. From the

logic of everyday situations both within and outside of the
murderous "service" itself, Goldhagen infers that the perpetrators must have had sufficient latitude for a reflective relation
to their own actions and involvement: "the perpetrators lived in
a world in which reflection, discussion, and disagreement were
possible".[5]

This leads Goldhagen to probe the question of what could
reasonably have been expected of the perpetrators: given the
circumstances, did they have no other choice but to act as they
did? Here Goldhagen points to killing operations that were
manned by volunteers, or which perpetrators undertook on
their own initiative; to declined offers to voluntarily excuse
themselves from participation in massacres; and to opportunities on the scene to refrain from taking part in killing operations without the threat of punishment. The men also
understood that they could, if nothing else helped, ask to be
transferred to another position, and that they could even refuse
to follow orders without placing their own lives in danger.
"Superfluous" violence, or the excessively gruesome nature of
the killing operations (which Goldhagen describes for analytical
reasons) also speaks against the assumption that the perpetrators found themselves trapped in a state of coercion. Goldhagen believes that he can rule out other possible grounds for
excusing the perpetrators, such as the social-psychological
effects of group pressure, a habituation to state-sanctioned
mass criminality, or an unconscious attachment to state authority. There is a natural suspicion that this type of perpetrator may
have been unusually fixated on the authority of his superior
officers; Goldhagen refutes this too by pointing out instances
of opposition and open insubordination in other situations hav-
ing nothing to do with the murder of Jews. Nor does self-interest
seem to have been a decisive motivation. In any case, the pro-
position that corruption, ambition, or interest in professional
advancement played no decisive motivational role is important
for Goldhagen's argument; one confirmation for this assumption is the truly bizarre behavior of the teams of guards on the
death marches during the final days of the war. If these people
acted wilfully, without any drastic outward coercion or obvious
inner compulsion; if they did not even act on utilitarian grounds,

then we are confronted with a picture of perpetrators who lacked any awareness that they were committing an injustice.

Philosophically, Goldhagen's study is inspired by the idea that evil is not to be understood as sheer aggression as such, but rather as the kind of aggression which the perpetrators believe themselves to be justified in committing. Evil is *distorted* good. With a wealth of details, from the lack of concern for secrecy to obscene sessions of posing for photographic mementoes, Goldhagen argues that many of the perpetrators must have regarded their murderous acts as legitimate. But anyone who can appeal to his convictions in order to participate in an act that would count as criminal by any normal standard – indeed, in an act that must count as monstrousness itself – must have some powerful normative basis to justify such a dramatic exception. Here Goldhagen naturally refers back to the conception of "the Jew." Since he is obliged to reconstruct the bases of the morally selective perception of the perpetrators from their visible acts, he collects evidence of the markedly differential treatment of designated victims. The antisemitic syndrome expresses itself in the fact that, in comparable situations, Jews consistently met a worse fate than Poles, Russians, political prisoners, and others. The perpetrators behaved more cruelly towards Jews than towards their other victims. As the current discussion on the Berlin Holocaust memorial continues, anyone inclined to mock the wish of survivors for a memorial that distinguishes between different victims should pause to remember who it was who first set up this "hierarchy of victim groups." Following this path, Goldhagen reaches his central contention: in the end, antisemitic conceptions explain the murderous actions of these perpetrators.

The concluding step of the argument is supported by a fact already suggested in the title of the exemplary study by Christopher Browning: the perpetrators were in fact "quite ordinary men."[6] Goldhagen sharpens this thesis concerning "ordinary Germans": with the help of the usual social-statistical analytical tools, he documents that the composition of Police Battalion 101 was roughly representative of the male population of Germany at the time. Naturally, retrospectively determined data of this sort cannot simply be equated with data derived from public opinion research. This is why serious qualifications are needed before one treats this police battalion as a representative sample, and draws the conclusion "that millions of other Germans would have behaved no differently had they found themselves in the same situation".[7] In the present context, it should be emphasized that such a conclusion ought not to lead us to adopt the stigmatizing reproach that the Germans were a "nation of murderers",[8] or only "potential murderers." Such counterfactual moral accusations are meaningless. Face to face, moral reproach can refer only to concrete, factual actions or omissions. But Goldhagen's counterfactual considerations quite reasonably relate to the undisputed and widespread antisemitic dispositions of the German population during this historical period.

III

The question of the rootedness of antisemitism in German culture during this period transcends the boundaries of any case study. Goldhagen is obliged to expand the scope of his analysis, from the already considerable number of perpetrators to the vast number of those whose involvement was indirect. From 1933 onward the Jewish population was systematically excluded from every sphere of German society, a process that was carried out in full public view. This would not have been possible without the silent complicity of broader strata of the German population. Referring to social elites, Goldhagen justly asks:

> How many German churchmen in the 1930s did not believe that the Jews were pernicious?...How many generals...did not want to cleanse Germany of the Jews?...How many jurists, how many in the medical community, how many in other professions held the ubiquitous, public antisemitism, with its hallucinatory elements, to be sheer nonsense?...To be sure, not all churchmen, generals, jurists and others wanted to exterminate the Jews. Some wanted to deport them, a few wanted to sterilize them, and some would have been content to deprive

the Jews "only" of fundamental rights. Nevertheless, underlying
all of these views was an eliminationist ideal.[9]

The only objection that comes to my mind is that Goldhagen
forgot the German professors.

On the other hand, these facts are not sufficient to justify
speaking of the extermination of the Jews as a "national project
of the Germans." Goldhagen himself refers to the medium of
"society's conversation," in which all of these eliminationist
intentions had to be articulated. The intersubjective constitution and the dynamics of public communication demand a
more differentiated picture. Even under the asymmetrical conditions of dictatorship, beliefs gain credence only in competition with other beliefs; cognitive models only against other
cognitive models. But the primary focus of the objections of
professional historians is the polemical thesis of a "direct road
to Auschwitz."[10] The impression that Goldhagen's intention-
alist argument overextends the credit of his empirical work by
drawing global explanations from it can be countered by Goldhagen himself, who firmly refuses monocausal explanations and
insists on a comparative approach. Goldhagen of course understands that in finding explanations for the Holocaust, one
"[cannot] limit one's self to antisemitism alone, but [must]
deal with countless other factors."[11] Any non-historian who
has familiarized himself with the range of controversies in the
broad field of Nazi research, reading Ian Kershaw[12] comes away
with the impression that competing interpretive approaches
tend to complement rather than contradict one another.

But it is not my job to offer a professional judgment on these
matters. On the present occasion, we are evaluating the contributions that an American, a Jewish, historian has made to
Germans' search for the proper way to come to terms with a
criminal period of their history. In conclusion I want to consider
a proposal that the legal theorist Klaus Günther has made for
the problem of how to cope in public with the history of
political crimes. How we decide questions of accountability
for crimes not only depends on the facts, but also on how we
view the facts. How much responsibility we ascribe to persons
and how much to historical circumstances, where we draw the

boundaries between individual freedom and constraint, guilt, and innoncence – these decisions depend on the particular pre-understanding with which we approach the events. The hermeneutic ability to recognize the true scope of responsibility and complicity for crime varies with our understanding of free-dom: how we value ourselves as persons, and how much we expect from ourselves as political actors. An ethical-political discourse of collective self-understanding raises just this pre-understanding as a topic of discussion. How we see the distri-bution of guilt and innocence in the past also reflects the pre-sent norms according to which we are willing to accord one another mutual respect as citizens of this Republic. And histor-ians who participate in this discourse do so no longer as experts, but, like us, in the role of intellectuals.

Here is where I see Goldhagen's real contribution. He is not arguing for supposed anthropological universals or regularities to which all persons are equally subjected. Such regularities may well serve to explain a portion of the unspeakable, as some comparative research in genocide maintains. Goldhagen's work, however, refers to very specific traditions and mental-ities, to ways of thinking and perceiving that belong to a particular cultural context – not something unalterable to which we have been consigned by fate, but factors that can be transformed through a change of consciousness, and which in the meantime *have* actually been transformed through political enlightenment. The union of anthropological pessimism and a fatalistic kind of historicism in this country is in fact a part of the very problem whose solution it pretends to offer. Daniel Goldhagen deserves our thanks for strengthening our ability to take *another* view of the past.

3

Learning from Catastrophe?

A Look Back at the Short Twentieth Century

I. The Long Rhythms of the Century

The threshold of the twenty-first century exerts such a strong grip on our imagination because it also leads us into a new millennium. This calendrical turning point is itself the product of a construction of religious history, whose starting point, the birth of Christ, marked what we recognize in hindsight as a break in world history. At the end of the second millennium, the timetables of international airlines, global stock market transactions, international scientific conventions, even rendez-vous in space are all scheduled according to the Christian calendar. But the round numbers that punctuate this calendar don't match up with the plots of historical events themselves. Years like 1900 or 2000 are meaningless in comparison to dates such as 1914, 1945, or 1989. What's more, these calendrical blocs can often have the effect of concealing the very continuity of far-reaching social trends, many of which have origins well before the beginning of the twentieth century and will continue well into the new millennium. Before beginning this examination of the physiognomy of the twentieth century, then, I will recall some of these longer rhythms that pass through the century. Here I will mention (a) demographic changes, (b) structural changes in the nature of employment, and (c) the course of development of science and technology.

(a) Europe's dramatic increase in population had its beginnings in the early nineteenth century. Largely a result of medical progress, this demographic change has in the meantime largely come to a standstill in affluent societies; in the Third World population growth has exploded since the middle of the twentieth century. Expert opinions do not expect a stabilization of world population – at a level of roughly 10 billion people – before 2030. That would be a fivefold increase in global population since 1950. Of course, a highly complicated phenomenology hides behind this statistical trend.

At the beginning of the twentieth century, the population explosion was described by contemporaries in terms of the social form of "the masses." Even then, the phenomenon was not an entirely new one. Well before Le Bon became interested in the "psychology of the mass," nineteenth-century novelists were already well acquainted with mass concentrations of people in cities, housing blocks, factory buildings, offices, and barracks, as well as with the mass mobilization of workers and immigrants, demonstrators, strikers, and revolutionaries. But it was not until the beginning of the twentieth century that massive flows of people, mass organizations, and mass actions began to appear intrusive enough to give rise to the vision of the "revolt of the masses" (Ortega y Gasset). The mass mobilizations of the Second World War, the mass misery of the concentration camps, mass treks of refugees, and the mass chaos of displaced persons after 1945 all exhibit a kind of collectivism first anticipated in the illustrated title page of Hobbes' *Leviathan*: countless individuals anonymously fused into the overpowering figure of a macro-subject of collective action. Since mid-century, however, the physiognomy of persons in great numbers has itself undergone a change. The presence of bodies – collected, herded together, set in motion – has given way to the symbolic inclusion of the consciousness of the many into ever wider networks of communication: the concentrated masses have been transformed into a broadly dispersed public of the mass media. Physical commercial flows, and commercial jams, keep rising; people massing in the streets and squares become anachronistic as individual connections are integrated into electronic networks. Of course, this change in social perception does not touch on the basic continuity of population growth.

(b) Similarly, structural changes in the labor system ignore the thresholds of centuries or millennia. The introduction of labor-saving production methods, and the subsequent increase in productivity, is the driving force behind these structural changes. Since the Industrial Revolution in eighteenth-century England, economic modernization has followed the same sequence in all countries. First, the mass of the laboring population is shifted into the secondary sectors of manufacturing industries from the primary agricultural work that had occupied them for millennia. Next they shift to the tertiary sectors of commerce, transportation, and services. Postindustrial societies are now characterized by a quarternary sector of knowledge-based economic activities such as high-tech industries or the health-care sector, banking or public administration, all of which depend on the influx of new information and, ultimately, on research and innovation. And research and innovation, in turn, are supported by an "educational revolution" (Talcott Parsons) which not only eliminated illiteracy but triggered a drastic expansion of systems of secondary and higher education. As higher education lost its elite status, the universities frequently became crucibles of political unrest.

Over the course of the twentieth century the pattern of these structural changes remained invariant, while its pace accelerated. Under a developmental dictatorship, a country like South Korea has, since 1960, succeeded in making the jump from a preindustrial to a postindustrial society within the space of a single generation. This acceleration explains the new quality that a well-established process of migration from countryside to urban areas assumed in the second half of the twentieth century: leaving aside sub-Saharan Africa and China, the soaring productivity caused by mechanized agriculture has all but depopulated the agrarian sector. In the OECD* countries, the proportion of labor engaged in heavily subsidized agriculture has fallen below 10 percent of the laboring population.

* Organization for Economic Cooperation and Development.

Counted in the phenomenological currency of lifeworld experiences, this signifies a truly radical break with the past. The mode of village life, which had been formative for all cultures from the neolithic period until well into the nineteenth century, survives only in imitation form in developed countries. The decline of the peasantry has also revolutionized the traditional relationship between the urban and the rural. Today, more than 40 percent of the world's population live in cities. The urbanization process, as it destroys the older forms of urban life that had arisen in premodern Europe, also destroys the city itself. If New York, even its metropolitan center in Manhattan, is itself already no more than vaguely reminiscent of the great cities of the nineteenth century such as London or Paris, then the sprawling urban areas of Mexico City, Tokyo, Calcutta, Sao Paulo, Seoul, or Shanghai have finally exploded the familiar dimensions of "the city." The hazy profiles of these megalopolises, where explosive growth is only two or three decades old, face us with a mode of experience that we are at a loss to comprehend.

(c) Finally, the series of social consequences of scientific and technological progress constitutes a third continuity extending through the twentieth century. New synthetic materials and energy sources, new industrial, military, and medical technologies, new means of transportation and communication have all revolutionized modes of human interaction and forms of life, but are all based on scientific knowledge and technical developments from the past. Technological triumphs such as the mastery of atomic energy and manned space travel, or innovations like the deciphering of the genetic code and the introduction of genetic technology into agriculture and medicine, surely change our awareness of risks; they even touch upon our ethical self-understanding. But in a certain sense, even these spectacular achievements have run along familiar lines. Since the seventeenth century, the instrumental attitude toward a scientifically objectified nature has not changed; nor has the manner in which we control natural processes, even if our interventions into matter are deeper, and our ventures into space are further, than ever before.

Technologically permeated structures of the lifeworld still require from us laypersons the banal, routinized mode of handling and operating machines and devices that we don't understand; a habitualized trust in the functioning of ongoing technologies and processes. In complex societies, every expert is a layperson in relation to other experts. Max Weber had already described the "second naïveté" that emerges as we busy ourselves with our radios and cell phones, our calculators, video gear, or laptops – with the operation of familiar electronic equipment whose manufacture requires the accumulated knowledge of generations of scientists. Despite all the panicky reactions to warnings, prognostications, and mishaps, the lifeworld's capacity to assimilate the strange and uncomprehended into the familiar can only be temporarily undermined by media-sponsored doubts about the reliability of expert knowledge and high technology. A growing awareness of risks does not disrupt the daily routine.

The acceleration effects of improved transport and communication technologies have an entirely different relevance for the long-term transformation of everyday experience. As early as 1830, travelers on the earliest railways described a new mode of perception of space and time. In the twentieth century, motor traffic and civil aviation accelerated the transport of persons and goods still further, shrinking the subjective sense of distance even more. Space and time consciousness were also affected by new technologies of information processing, storage, and retrieval. Late eighteenth-century Europe already saw the new print media of books and newspapers contribute to the emergence of a global, future-oriented historical consciousness; at the end of the nineteenth century Nietzsche complained of the historicism of an educated elite that brought everything past into the present. Since then, the thoroughgoing decoupling of the present from the objectified pasts of museums has reached the masses of educational tourists. The mass print media is a child of the twentieth century too; but the time-machine effect of the print media was intensified over the course of the century through photography, film, radio, and television. Spatial and temporal distances are not "conquered" any more. They vanish without trace into the ubiquitous

present of virtual realities. Digital communication finally sur-
passes all other media in scope and capacity. More people have
quicker access to greater volumes of information, and are able
to process it and instantly exchange it over any distance. The
mental consequences of the Internet – which is proving much
more resistant to incorporation into the routines of the lifeworld than a new electronic gadget – are still very hard to assess.

II. Two Physiognomies of the Century

The continuities of social modernization extending through the
century can only inadequately teach us what is characteristic of
the twentieth century *as such*. Thus historians tend to punctuate the historical flow of their narratives with events, rather
than trends and structural transformations. And indeed the
physiognomy of a century is molded by the caesurae of great
events. Among those historians who are still willing to think in
terms of large historical units, a consensus has emerged that the
"long" nineteenth century (1789–1914) is followed by a
"short" twentieth century (1914 89). The outbreak of the
First World War and the collapse of the Soviet Union thus
frame an antagonism that stretches through both world wars
and the Cold War. Of course, this punctuation permits three
very different interpretations, depending on where one locates
this antagonism – on the economic level of social systems, on
the political level of superpowers, or on the cultural level of
ideologies. Which hermeneutical viewpoint is chosen is, naturally enough, itself determined by a conflict of ideas that has
dominated the century.

The Cold War is carried on today by historiographic means,
whether the terms of the conflict are described as the Soviet
Union's challenge to the capitalist West (Eric Hobsbawm), or
the struggle of the liberal West against totalitarian regimes
(François Furet). Both interpretations explain in one way or
another the fact that only the United States emerged from the
world wars in a politically, economically, and culturally
strengthened position, and from the Cold War as the world's

only superpower, an outcome that has labeled the twentieth century "the American century." The third reading of the Cold War is more ambiguous. As long as "ideology" is employed in a neutral sense, the title *The Age of Ideologies* (Hildebrand) expresses nothing more than a variant of a theory of totalitarianism, according to which the struggle of regimes reflects a struggle of contending ideologies. But in another sense, the same title signals the claim (developed by Carl Schmitt) that since 1917 the mutually opposed utopian projects of world democracy and world revolution, with Wilson and Lenin as their exponents, have engaged one another in a global civil war (Ernst Nolte). According to this ideology critique from the Right, 1917 marks the point where history became infected with the bacillus of the philosophy of history, and was so badly derailed that it was not until 1989 that it was able to jump back onto the normal tracks of pristine national histories.

Each of these three perspectives endows the short twentieth century with a distinctive physiognomy. According to the first reading, the century is driven by the challenge presented to the capitalist world system by the single largest experiment ever conducted on human beings: carried out with extreme brutality and at the cost of enormous sacrifice, the forced industrialization of the Soviet Union certainly set the course for its rise to the status of a superpower, but it also left the Soviet Union without a sound economic and social-political basis on which to construct a superior, or even a viable, alternative to the Western model. The second reading sees the century under the shadow of a totalitarianism that broke entirely with the civilizing forces ushered in by the Enlightenment, destroying the hopes for a domestication of state power and a humanization of social relations. The boundless violence of regimes engaging in total war shatters the barriers of international law just as ruthlessly as the terrorist violence of single-party dictatorships neutralizes constitutional protections internally. These first two readings divide up light and shadow between the forces of totalitarianism and their liberal enemies clearly enough; for the third, post-fascist reading, the century stands overshadowed by an ideological crusade of parties whose mentalities are essentially similar, even if they are not of the same rank. Both sides appear to fight out the global contradictions between programs justified by differing philosophies of history; programs that owe their power to kindle fanaticism to essentially religious energies perverted to serve secular ends.

Notwithstanding all their differences, these three interpretations have one thing in common: they all oblige us to look at the gruesome features of a century that "invented" the gas chambers, total war, state-sponsored genocide and extermination camps, brainwashing, state security apparatuses, and the panoptic surveillance of entire populations. The twentieth century "generated" more victims, more dead soldiers, more murdered civilians, more displaced minorities, more torture, more dead from cold, from hunger, from maltreatment, more political prisoners and refugees, than could ever have been imagined. The phenomena of violence and barbarism mark the distinctive signature of the age. From Horkheimer and Adorno to Baudrillard, from Heidegger to Foucault and Derrida, the totalitarian features of the age have also embedded themselves into the very structure of its critical diagnoses. And this raises the question of whether these negativistic interpretations, by remaining transfixed by the gruesomeness of the century, might be missing the reverse side of all these catastrophes.

Of course, it took decades for those who were directly involved and affected to come to a conscious assessment of the dimensions of the horror that finally culminated in the Holocaust, in the methodical annihilation of the Jews of Europe. But even if it was suppressed at first, this shock eventually set loose energies, even opened new insights, that brought about a reversal in the perception of this horror during the second half of the century. For the nations that dragged the planet into a technologically unlimited war in 1914, and for the people who were forced to confront the mass crimes of an ideologically unlimited war of extermination after 1939, the year 1945 also marks a turning point – a turn toward something better, toward the mastering of the force of barbarism that had broken through the very foundations of civilization in Germany. Should we not have learned something from the catastrophes of the first half of the twentieth century?

My doubts regarding all three of these readings can be expressed in this way: the demarcation of a short twentieth century forces periods of global war and the Cold War period together into a single unit, suggesting the appearance of a homogenous, uninterrupted, 75-year war of systems, regimes, and ideologies. But this has the effect of occluding the very event that not only divides this century chronologically, but also constitutes an economic, political, and above all a normative watershed: the defeat of fascism. In the context of the Cold War, the ideological significance of the wartime alliance between the Western powers and the Soviet Union against the German *Reich* was dismissed as "unnatural" and promptly forgotten. But the Allied victory and the German defeat of 1945 permanently discredited an array of myths which, ever since the end of the nineteenth century, had been mobilized against the heritage of 1789. Allied victory not only sparked the democratic developments in the Federal Republic of Germany, Japan, and Italy, and eventually Portugal and Spain. It undermined the foundations of *all* forms of political legitimation that did not – at least verbally, at least in words – subscribe to the universalist spirit of political enlightenment. This is of course little consolation for victims of ongoing violations of human rights.

The year 1945 saw a change in the cultural and intellectual climate that formed a necessary condition for all three of the uncontested cultural innovations of this century. The revolutionary changes in the fine arts, architecture, and music that had begun in the decades before, during, and after the First World War, and which drew from the experience of war itself, attained worldwide recognition only after 1945, in the past tense, as it were, of "classical modernism." Until the early 1930s, avante-garde art produced a repertoire of entirely new aesthetic forms and techniques, opening a horizon of possibilities that was exploited but never transcended by the experiments of international art during the second half of the century. Only two philosophers, Heidegger and Wittgenstein – both opposed to the spirit of modernism, to be sure – possessed a comparable originality and exerted a comparable historical influence.

This changed cultural climate after 1945 also formed the background for the political developments which, according to Eric Hobsbawm,[1] changed the face of the postwar period until the 1980s: the Cold War (a), decolonialization (b), and the construction of the social welfare state (c).

(a) The continuing spiral of an arrogant, exhausting arms race certainly succeeded in keeping directly threatened nations in a state of continual fear. Nevertheless the mad calculations of a balance of terror – MAD was the self-ironic abbreviation for mutually assured destruction – did prevent the outbreak of a hot war. The unexpected, mutual concession of two super-powers gone wild – the eminently reasonable agreement that Reagan and Gorbachev reached in Reykjavik that introduced the end of the arms race – makes the Cold War appear in hindsight as a high-risk process of the self-domestication of nuclear alliances. This is also an apt description for the peaceful implosion of a global empire, whose leadership recognized the inefficiency of a supposedly superior mode of production, and admitted defeat in the economic race rather than following the time-honored pattern of deflecting internal conflicts with military adventures abroad.

(b) The process of decolonialization did not follow a straight path either. In hindsight, however, the colonial powers only fought rearguard actions. The French fought in vain against national liberation movements in Indochina; in 1956 Britain and France saw their military adventure in Suez end in failure. In 1975 the United States was forced to end its intervention in Vietnam after ten costly years of war. The year 1945 marked the end of Japan's colonial empire and the independence of Syria and Libya. Britain withdrew from India in 1947; Burma, Sri Lanka, Israel, and Indonesia were all founded in the following year. The western regions of the Islamic world from Iran to Morocco next gained independence, followed gradually by the states of Central Africa and finally the last remaining colonies in Southeast Asia and the Caribbean. The end of the apartheid regime in South Africa, and the return of Hong Kong and Macao to China, conclude a process that has at least formally ended the dependencies of colonial peoples and established new states (all too often torn by civil war, cultural conflicts, and ethnic strife) as equal members in the UN General Assembly.

(c) The third development is an unambiguous change for the better. In the affluent and peaceful Western European democracies, and to a lesser degree in the United States, Japan, and some other countries, mixed economies made possible the establishment and effective realization of basic social rights. Of course, the explosive growth of the global economy, the quadrupling of industrial production, and an exponential increase in world trade between the early 1950s and the early 1970s also generated disparities between the rich and the poor regions of the world. But the governments of the OECD nations, who were responsible for three-quarters of global production and four-fifths of global trade in industrial goods during these two decades, had learned enough from the catastrophic experiences of the period between the two world wars to pursue intelligent domestic economic policies, focussing on stability with a relatively high rate of economic growth, and on the construction and enhancement of comprehensive social security systems. In welfare-state mass democracies, highly productive capitalist economies were socially domesticated for the first time, and were thus brought more or less in line with the normative self-understanding of democratic constitutional states.

These three developments lead a Marxist historian such as Eric Hobsbawm to celebrate the postwar era as a "golden age." But since 1989 at the latest, there has been a growing public realization that this era is reaching its end. In countries where the social welfare state is still acknowledged as a positive achievement even in hindsight, there is a growing mood of resignation. The end of the twentieth century was marked by a structural threat to the welfarist domestication of capitalism, and by the revival of a socially reckless form of neoliberalism. Commenting on the current mood – somewhat depressed, somewhat clueless, the whole thing washed over by the throb of techno-pop – Hobsbawm could almost be taken for an author from late Roman antiquity: "The Short Twentieth

Century ended in problems, for which nobody had, or even claimed to have, solutions. As the citizens of the *fin-de-siècle* tapped their way through the global fog that surrounded them, into the third millenium, all they knew for certain was that an era of history had ended. They knew very little else.''[2]

Even the old problems – peacekeeping and international security, economic disparities between North and South, the risks of ecological catastrophe – were already global ones. But today these problems have all been sharpened by a newly emerging problem that supersedes the old challenges. Capitalism's new, apparently irrevocable globalizing dynamic drastically reduces the G7 states' freedom of action, which had enabled them, unlike the economically dependent states of the Third World, to hang on to a relative degree of independence. Economic globalization forms the central challenge for the political and social orders that grew out of postwar Europe (III). One way to meet this challenge would consist in strengthening the regulatory power of politics, to allow politics to catch up with global markets that are beyond the reach of nationstates (IV). Or does the lack of any clear orientation for ways of meeting this challenge indicate not that we *can* learn from catastrophes, but indeed that we *only* learn from catastrophes?

III. At the End of the Welfare-State Compromise

Ironically, developed societies in the twenty-first century are faced with the reappearance of a problem that they seemed to have only recently solved under the pressure of systemic competition. The problem is as old as capitalism itself: how to make the most effective use of the allocative and innovative functions of self-regulating markets, while simultaneously avoiding unequal patterns of distribution and other social costs that are incompatible with the conditions for social integration in liberal democratic states. In the mixed economies of the West, states had a considerable portion of the domestic product at their disposal, and could therefore use transfer payments, subsidies, and effective policies in the areas of infrastructure, employment, and social security. They were able to exert a definite influence on the overall conditions of production and distribution with the goal of maintaining growth, stable prices, and full employment. In other words, by applying growth-stimulating measures on the one side, and social policies on the other, the regulatory state could simultaneously stimulate the economy and guarantee social integration.

Notwithstanding the considerable differences between them, the social-political spheres in countries like the United States, Japan, and the Federal Republic of Germany saw continued expansion until the 1980s. Since then, this trend has been reversed in all OECD countries: benefits have been reduced, while at the same time access to social security has been tightened and the pressure on the unemployed has increased. The transformation and reduction of the social welfare state is the direct consequence of supply-side economic policies – anti-inflationary monetary and fiscal policies, the reduction of direct taxation, the transfer of state-owned enterprises into the private sector, and so on – aimed at deregulating markets, reducing subsidies, and creating a more favorable investment climate.

Of course, the consequence of the revocation of the welfare-state compromise is that the crisis tendencies it had previously counteracted now break out into open view. Emerging social costs threaten to overburden the integration capacities of liberal societies. The indicators of a rise in poverty and income disparities are unmistakable, as are the tendencies toward social disintegration.[3] The gap between the standard of living of the employed, the underemployed, and the unemployed is widening. "Underclasses" arise wherever exclusions – from the employment system, from higher education, from the benefits of transfer payments, from housing markets, from family resources, and so on – are compounded. Impoverished social groups, largely cordoned off from the broader society, can no longer improve their social position through their own efforts.[4] In the long run, a loss of solidarity such as this will inevitably destroy a liberal political culture whose universalistic self-understanding democratic societies depend on. Procedurally correct majority decisions that merely reflect the fears and self-defensive reactions of social classes threatened with downward mobility – decisions that reflect the sentiments of right-wing populism, in other words – will end up eroding the legitimacy of democratic procedures and institutions themselves.

Neoliberals, who are prepared to accept a higher level of social inequities, who even believe in the inherent fairness of "position valuations" via globalized financial markets, will naturally differ in their appraisal of this situation from those who recognize that equal social rights are the mainstays of democratic citizenship, and who thus still adhere to the "social-democratic age." But both sides describe the dilemma similarly. The gist of their diagnoses is that national governments have been forced into a zero-sum game where necessary economic objectives can be reached only at the expense of social and political objectives. In the context of a global economy, nation-states can only increase the international competitiveness of their "position" by imposing self-restrictions on the formative powers of the state itself. And this justifies the sort of "dismantling" policies that end up damaging social cohesion and social stability as such.[5] I cannot go into a full description of this dilemma here.[6] But it boils down to two theses: First, the economic problems besetting affluent societies can be explained by a structural transformation of the world economic system, a transformation characterized by the term "globalization." Second, this transformation so radically reduces nation-states' capacity for action that the options remaining open to them are not sufficient to shield their populations from the undesired social and political consequences of a transnational economy.[7]

The nation-state has fewer and fewer options open to it. Two of these options are now completely ruled out: protectionism, and the return to a demand-oriented economic policy. Insofar as the movement of capital can be controlled at all, the costs of a protectionist closure of domestic economies would quickly become intolerably high under the conditions of a global economy. And the failure of state employment programs today is not just due to limits on national domestic budgets; these programs are also simply no longer effective within the national framework. In a globalized economy, "Keynsianism in one's own country" just won't work any more. Policies that promote a proactive, intelligent, and sustainable adaptation of national conditions to global competition are much more promising. Such policies include familiar measures for a long-range industrial policy, support for research and development, improving the competitiveness of the workforce through retraining and continuing education, and a reasonable degree of "flexibility" for the labor market. For the middle term, measures such as these would produce locational advantages but would not fundamentally alter the pattern of international competition as such. No matter how one looks at it, the globalization of the economy destroys a historical constellation that made the welfare state compromise temporarily possible. Even if this compromise was never the ideal solution for a problem inherent within capitalism itself, it nevertheless held capitalism's social costs within tolerable limits.

Until the seventeenth century, emerging European states were defined by their sovereign rule over a specific territory; their enhanced steering capacities made these states superior to earlier political forms such as the ancient empires or city-states. As a functionally specialized administrative state, the modern state differentiated itself from the legally institutionalized private sphere of a market economy; at the same time, as a tax-based state, it grew dependent on a capitalist economy. Over the course of the nineteenth century, now in the form of the nation-state, the modern state began for the first time to open itself to democratic forms of legitimation. In some privileged regions of the world, and under the favorable conditions of the postwar period, the nation-state – which had in the meantime established the worldwide model for political organization – succeeded in transforming itself into a social welfare state by regulating the national economy without interfering with its self-correcting mechanisms. But this successful combination is menaced by a global economy that now increasingly escapes the control of a regulatory state. Obviously, welfare-state functions can be maintained at their previous level only if they are transferred from the nation-state to larger political entities which could manage to keep pace with a transnational economy.

IV. Beyond the Nation-State?

For this reason, the focus is on the construction of supranational institutions. Continent-wide economic alliances such as NAFTA or APEC let national governments enter into binding agreements, or at least agreements that are backed by mild sanctions. The benefits of cooperation are greater for more ambitious projects such as the European Union. Continent-wide regimes of this sort can establish unified currency zones that help reduce the risk of fluctuating exchange rates, but, more significantly, they can also create larger political entities with a hierarchical organization of competencies. In the future, we will have to decide whether we want to rely on the status quo of a Europe that remains integrated only through markets, or whether we want to set a course for a European democracy.[8]

Of course, even a geographically and economically expanded regime of this sort would at best still generate internal advantages for global competition, and would thus enhance its position against other regimes. The creation of larger political entities leads to defensive alliances against the rest of the world, but it changes nothing in the mode of locational competition as such. It does not, *per se*, bring about a change of course that would replace various adaptations to the transnational economic system with an attempt to influence the overall context of the economic system itself. On the other hand, expanded political alliances are a necessary condition if politics are to catch up with the forces of a globalized economy. With the emergence of each new supranational entity, the overall number of political actors grows smaller, but the club of those very few actors capable of global action, or capable of cooperation, gains a new member. Given the required political will, such actors will be in the position to enter into binding agreements that will set up a basic framework for a globalized economy.

Given all the difficulties of creating a European Union, an agreement for the creation of a worldwide order – especially one that would not simply exhaust itself in creating and legally institutionalizing markets, but would introduce elements of a global political will-formation, and would work toward redressing the undesired social consequences of global commerce – would be much more difficult. As nation-states are increasingly overwhelmed by the global economy, one clear alternative emerges, even if somewhat abstractly and viewed, so to speak, from the academic ivory tower: transferring functions that social welfare states had previously exercised at the national level onto supranational authorities. At this supranational level, however, there is no mode of political coordination that would both guide market-driven transnational commerce and maintain social standards. Of course, the world's 191 sovereign states are bound together in a thick network of institutions subsisting below the level of the United Nations.[9] Approximately 350 intergovernmental organizations, half of which were created after 1960, serve a variety of economic, social, and peacekeeping functions. But these organizations are naturally in no position to exercise any positive political coordination, or to fulfill any regulatory functions in areas of social, economic, or labor policy that are relevant for questions of redistribution.

Nobody wants to spin out utopian fantasies; certainly not these days when all utopian energies seem to be exhausted.[10] Without some significant effort on the part of the social sciences, the idea of supranational politics "catching up" with markets cannot even attain the status of a "project." Such a project would, at the very least, need to be guided by examples where differing interest positions are equalized in a way that all involved could find reasonable, and it would need to sketch the outlines for a range of unified procedures and practices. Social science's resistance to the project of a transnational regime along the lines of a world domestic policy is understandable if we assume that such a project could only be justified by the given interest positions of existing states and their populations, and put in place by independent political powers. In a stratified world society, unredeemable conflicts of interest seem to result from the asymmetrical interdependencies between developed nations, newly industrialized nations, and the less developed nations. But this perception is only correct as long as there are no institutionalized procedures of transnational will-formation that could induce globally competent actors to broaden their individual preferences into a "global governance."[11]

Globalization processes are not just economic. Bit by bit, they introduce us to *another* perspective, from which we see the growing interdependence of social arenas, communities of risks, and the networks of shared fate ever more clearly. The acceleration and the intensification of communication and commerce shrink spatial and temporal distances; expanding markets run up against the limits of the planet; the exploitation of resources meets the limits of nature. These narrowed horizons rule out the option of externalizing the consequences of many of our actions: it is increasingly rare that costs and risks can be shifted onto others – whether other sectors of society, other geographical regions, other cultures, or future generations – without sanctions of one kind or another. This fact is as obvious for the risks of large-scale technologies, which can no longer be localized, as it is for affluent societies' production of toxic wastes, which now endanger every part of the earth.[12] But how much longer will we be able to shift social costs onto the "superfluous" segment of the working population?

International agreements and regulations aimed at counteracting such externalizations of costs can certainly not be expected from governments as long as they are perceived as independent actors controlling their own national arenas, where governments must always secure the support of (and reelection by) their populations. The incorporation of each individual state into the binding cooperative procedures of a cosmopolitan community of states would have to be perceived as a part of states' own domestic policies. Thus the decisive question is whether the civil society and the political public sphere of increasingly large regimes can foster the consciousness of an obligatory cosmopolitan solidarity. Only the transformed consciousness of citizens, as it imposes itself in areas of domestic policy, can pressure global actors to change their own self-understanding sufficiently to begin to see themselves as members of an international community who are compelled to cooperate with one another, and hence to take one another's interests into account. And this change in perspective from "international relations" to a world domestic policy cannot be expected from ruling elites until the population itself, on the basis of its own understanding of its own best interests, rewards them for it.[13]

An encouraging example of this is the pacifist consciousness that had clearly developed in the wake of two barbaric world wars in the nations that were directly involved, and which subsequently spread to many other countries. We know that this change of consciousness did not prevent further regional wars, or countless civil wars in other parts of the world. But it did bring about a change in the political and cultural parameters of interstate relations large enough for the UN Declaration of Human Rights, with its prohibition against wars of aggression and crimes against humanity, to gain the weak normative binding force of a publicly recognized convention. This is not enough, of course, for the institutionalization of the economic procedures, practices, and regulations that could solve the problems of economic globalization. An effective regulation of a world society demands policies that successfully redistribute burdens. And that will be possible only on the basis of a cosmopolitan solidarity that is still lacking; a solidarity that would certainly be weaker and less binding than the civil solidarity that developed within nation-states. The human population has long since coalesced into an unwilling community of shared risk. Under this pressure, it is thus quite plausible that the great, historically momentous dynamic of abstraction from local, to dynastic, to national to democratic consciousness would take one more step forward.

The institutionalization of procedures for global coordination and generalization of interests, and for the imaginative construction of common interests, will not work in the organizational form of a world state; a form that is itself not even desirable. The autonomy, particularity, and uniqueness of formerly sovereign states will have to be taken into account. But what sort of path will take us there? The Hobbesian problem – how to create a stable social order – overtaxes the cooperative capacities of rational egoists, even on the global level. Institutional innovations come out of societies whose political elites find a resonance and support for them in the already transformed basic value orientations of their populations. Thus the first addressees for this "project" are not governments. They are social movements and non-governmental organizations; the active members of a civil society that stretches beyond national borders. The idea that the regulatory power of politics has to grow to catch up with globalized markets, in any event, refers to the complex relationships between the coordinative capacities of political regimes, on the one hand, and on the other a new mode of integration: cosmopolitan solidarity.

4

The Postnational Constellation and the Future of Democracy

All politicians move to the center to compete on the basis of
personality and of who is best able to manage the adjustment in
economy and society necessary to sustain competitiveness in the
global market . . . The concept of a possible alternative economy
and society is excluded.

Robert Cox, 1997

In 1929, Siegfried Landshut published a remarkable work
entitled *Critique of Sociology*. In it, he developed the thesis
that sociology only comes to construct its object of study,
"society," by adopting a particular perspective. The philosophical formulation of the question of rational law – the question
of how an association of free and equal citizens can be constructed through the means of positive law – forms the emancipatory horizon of expectation within which the resistance to
what appears as an unreasonable reality becomes visible. This
becomes the vision of sociology as well. In Hegel's *Philosophy of
Right* this connection is still clear: describing "civil society" as
"ethical life lost in its extremes," Hegel gives an entirely new,
modern meaning to a classical conception. Following the development of this conception from Hegel via Marx and Lorenz von
Stein to Max Weber, Landshut shows how sociology, as it gradually loses the Hegelian belief in the rationality of the real, also
covers the traces of its own history. Ultimately sociology con-

ceals that form of normative expectation through which
"society" – as distinguished from "state" – first appeared as the
sum total of the causal determinants of inequality and domination. But sociology still has to come to terms with the disappointment over the "impotence" of the obligatory moment of
natural law: " 'Society' is nothing more than the title meant to
encompass the tensions, contradictions, and ambiguities that
arise from the realization of the ideals of freedom and equality."[1]

Margaret Thatcher – the first genuinely "postmodern" poli-
tician – must have had some intuitive understanding of this
situation when she hit upon the slogan that "there is no such
thing as society." In the political public sphere, conflicts on a
national, European, or global scale develop their power to dis-
turb us only when they are seen, against the background of a
normative understanding of social inequities and political
oppression, not as natural phenomena but as social products –
hence as changeable. But since 1989, more and more politicians
seem to be saying: if we can't solve any of these conflicts, let's at
least dim the critical insights that turn conflicts into challenges.

The million people living below the official poverty line in the
Federal Republic of Germany, along with the 2.7 million who
receive some form of social aid, are a political challenge. The
fact that the increase in seasonally adjusted monthly figures for
registered unemployment coincides with higher and higher
levels of share prices and corporate earnings is a political challenge. The fact that criminal acts with a right-wing extremist
element have increased by a third over the last year is a political
challenge. The widening gap in living standards between the
prosperous North and the impoverished, chaotic, and self-
destructive regions of the South, or the looming cultural conflicts between a largely secularized West and a fundamentalist
Islamic world, or the sociocentric traditions of the Far East, are
political challenges – to say nothing of the warning signals from
the relentlessly ticking ecological clock; the balkanization of
regions collapsing into civil wars and ethnic conflicts, and so on.[2]

The list of problems that confront anybody who reads a
newspaper these days can, of course, only change into a political
agenda for a public which maintains a degree of trust in the
possibility of a conscious transformation of society – and which

can in turn be entrusted with it. The diagnosis of social conflicts transforms itself into a list of just as many political challenges only if we attach a further premise to the egalitarian institutions of rational law: the assumption that the unified citizens of a democratic community are able to shape their own social environment and can develop the capacity for action necessary for such interventions to succeed. The legal concept of self-legislation has to acquire a political dimension: it must be broadened to include the concept of a society capable of a democratic mode of self-direction and self-intervention. This is the only way that existing constitutions can be interpreted in terms of the reformist project of the realization of the "just" or "well-ordered" society.[3] In postwar Europe, this dynamic reading of the democratic process served as a guide for politicians across the political spectrum as they constructed social welfare states. And conversely, the very success of this social-democratic project, as one could call it, has nourished the vision of a society capable of conscious change through the will of its democratically united citizens.

The welfare-state mass democracies on the Western model now face the end of a 200-year developmental process that began with the revolutionary birth of modern nation-states. We should recall this beginning if we want to understand why the welfare state has fallen on such hard times. The counterfactual content of the idea of republican autonomy, as it was developed by Rousseau and Kant, was able to triumph over its many detractors only by establishing its "headquarters" in societies constituted as nation-states. The phenomena of the territorial state, the nation, and a popular economy constituted within national borders formed a historical constellation in which the democratic process assumed a more or less convincing institutional form.[4] And the idea that one part of a democratic society is capable of a reflexive intervention into society as a whole has, until now, been realized only in the context of nation-states. Today, developments summarized under the term "globalization" have put this entire constellation into question.

It is a paradoxical situation. We perceive the trends toward a postnational constellation as a list of political challenges only because we still describe them from the familiar perspective of the nation-state. But the more aware of this situation we become, the more our democratic self-confidence is shaken; a confidence that is necessary if conflicts are to be perceived as challenges, as problems awaiting a political solution: "For if state sovereignty is no longer conceived as indivisible but shared with international agencies; if states no longer have control over their national territories; and if territorial and political boundaries are increasingly permeable, the core principles of democratic liberty – that is self-governance, the demos, consent, representation, and popular sovereignty – are made distinctly problematic."[5]

The idea that societies are capable of democratic self-control and self-realization has until now been credibly realized only in the context of the nation-state. Thus the image of a postnational constellation gives rise to alarmist feelings of enlightened helplessness widely observed in the political arena today. There is a crippling sense that national politics have dwindled to more or less intelligent management of a process of forced adaptation to the pressure to shore up purely local positional advantages. It is a perception that deprives political controversies of their last bit of substance. The much-lamented "Americanization" of electoral campaigns reflects a situation so troubled that it seems to rule out any comprehensive overview.

One alternative to the forced cheerfulness of a "self-dismantling" neoliberal politics would consist in finding the appropriate forms for the democratic process to take *beyond* the nation-state. Under the pressure of de-nationalization, societies constituted as nation-states are "opening" themselves to an economically driven world society. What interests me is the desirability, and, under present circumstances, the possibility, of a renewed political "closure" of this global society. What would a political response to the challenges of the postnational constellation look like?

I will begin by recalling the classical features and underlying presuppositions of the nation-state, and then elaborate on the events associated with the term "globalization." (I) This background will show how the transformed constellation we are currently witnessing touches on the most basic functions and legitimacy conditions of democratic nation-states. (II) Sweeping responses to the perceived loss of nation-states' capacities for action certainly do not go far enough. The question of whether politics can and should "catch up" with global markets requires that we keep in mind the balance between the opening and the closure of socially integrated forms of life. (III) I will develop the alternative to an unreflective adaptation to the imperatives of "locational competition" in two steps: first in regard to the future of the European Union (IV), and then in terms of a potential global domestic policy, which could affect the terms of local competition itself (V).

I

Although many states to this day bear features reminiscent of ancient empires (China), city-states (Singapore), theocracies (Iran), or tribal organizations (Kenya), or betray features of family clans (El Salvador) or multinational concerns (Japan), the members of the "United Nations Organization" neverthe-less form an association of nation-states. The form of national organization that emerged from the American and French re-volutions has successfully spread over the entire world. Not all nation-states were, or are, democratic; that is, constituted according to the principles of an association of self-governing free and equal citizens. But wherever democracies on the West-ern model have appeared, they have done so in the form of the nation-state. Clearly, the nation-state fulfills important precon-ditions for societies constituted within determinate borders to exert a democratic form of self-control. The construction of the democratic process within the nation-state form can be schem-atically analyzed under four aspects: the emergence of the state in its modern form as an administrative state supported through taxation (a); maintaining sovereignty over a determinate geo-graphical territory (b); in the specific form of the nation-state (c), which then democratically developed into a legal and social state (d).[6]

(a) Before a society can effectively intervene in its own course, it must first develop a subsystem that specializes in producing

collectively binding decisions. The *administrative state*, constituted in the form of positive law, can be seen as the product of
such a functional specialization. The separation of state and
society also means the differentiation of a market economy
institutionalized via the principles of individual private rights.
The individualistic model of the legal system reflects a functional imperative of self-regulating markets, which depend on
the decentralized decisions of market participants. Law is not
merely an organizational medium for the purposes of administration. It also shields a privatized society from the state, insofar
as it steers the interaction between state and society along legal
tracks. In this sense, the modern state can be understood as a
legal state. The separation of the functional spheres of politics
and economy has two important consequences. On the one
hand, the most important regulatory powers of public administration remain reserved for the state, which maintains a
monopoly on the legitimate use of force. On the other hand,
a functionally specified public administrative power – the
state's power to levy taxes – depends on resources generated
by economic activity delegated to the private sphere.

(b) The "self-control" of society presupposes a well-defined
"self" of an appropriate magnitude. The idea of society as a
network of interactions, extended in space and time, is not
specific enough. The conception of a "democratic" self-control
of society implies rational law's conception of a determinate
number of persons, united by the decision to grant one another
precisely those rights that are necessary for the legitimate ordering of their collective existence through the means of positive
law.[7] However, the conditions for a successful implementation
of positive, compulsory law require that the social delimitation
of the political community has to be combined with the territorial delimitation of the geographical area that will be under the
control of a state. Because a state's territory will encompass the
sphere of validity for a state-sanctioned legal order, membership
in a state must be defined territorially. Within the borders of the
territorial state the population of a state is defined as the potential subjects of self-legislation, as democratically united citizens,
while society is defined as the potential object of their control.

The territorial principle, furthermore, underlies the separation of international relations from the sphere of state sovereignty: foreign and domestic policy follow different sets of premises. Externally, as opposed to all the other subjects of international law, the state justifies its sovereignty by its right to maintain the integrity of mutually recognized borders. This prohibition against foreign intervention does not exclude the *jus ad bellum*, that is, the "right" of a state to wage war. The status of state sovereignty is assured by the factually established autonomy of state power, and is measured by the state's capacity to protect its borders against external threats and to maintain "law and order" internally.

(c) Democratic self-determination can only come about if the population of a state is transformed into a nation of citizens who take their political destiny into their own hands. The political mobilization of "subjects," however, depends on a prior cultural integration of what is initially a number of people who have been thrown together with each other. This desideratum is fulfilled by the idea of the nation, with whose help the members of a state construct a new form of collective identity beyond their inherited loyalties to village, family, place, or clan. The cultural symbolism of "a people" secures its own particular character, its "spirit of the people," in the presumed commonalities of descent, language, and history, and in this way generates a unity, even if only an imaginary one. It thereby makes the residents of a single state-controlled territory aware of a collective belonging that, until then, had been merely abstract and legal. Only the symbolic construction of "a people" makes the modern state into a nation-state.

Constructed through the medium of modern law, the modern territorial state thus depends on the development of a national consciousness to provide it with the cultural substrate for a civil solidarity. With this solidarity, the bonds that had formed between members of a concrete community on the basis of personal relationships now change into a new, more abstract form. While remaining strangers to one another, members of the same "nation" feel responsible enough for one another that they are prepared to make "sacrifices" – as in military service or the burden of redistributive taxation. In the Federal Republic of Germany, financial redistribution between federal states is an example of the willingness of citizens to stand up for one another; a willingness that an egalitarian, universalistic legal order expects from its citizens.

(d) The association of free and equal legal persons is completed only with a democratic mode for the legitimation of political authority. Regarded as an ideal type, the change from princely to popular sovereignty also transforms the rights of "subjects" into the rights of human beings and citizens: into liberal and political civil rights, which guarantee both private and political autonomy. The democratic constitutional state, by its own definition, is a political order created by the people themselves and legitimated by their opinion- and will-formation, which allows the addressees of law to regard themselves at the same time as the authors of the law. But because capitalism follows a logic of its own, it is unable to conform to these demanding premises by itself: politics must see to it that the social conditions for public and private autonomy are met. Otherwise an essential condition for the legitimacy of democracy is endangered.

No systematic disadvantages or discriminations may be permitted that deprive members of underprivileged groups of the chance to make actual use of formal rights allocated on the basis of equality. The dialectic of legal equality and factual inequality[8] gives rise to the social welfare state, whose principal goal is to secure the social, technological, and ecological conditions that make an equal opportunity for the use of equally distributed basic rights possible. Social state interventionism, itself justified by these basic rights, expands the democratic self-legislation of the citizens of a nation-state into the democratic self-steering of a national-state society.

In postwar Europe, the democratic process has been more or less firmly institutionalized under the four aspects I have described. Since the end of the 1970s, however, this form of national-state institutionalization has come under increasing pressure from the force of globalization. I use the concept of "globalization" here to describe a process, not an end-state. It characterizes the increasing scope and intensity of commercial, communicative, and exchange relations beyond national borders. Just as the railroad, steamship, and telegraph intensified and accelerated the flow of goods, persons, and information in the nineteenth century, so today satellite technology, air travel, and digitalized communication have the effect of expanding and intensifying networks. "Network" has emerged as a key term, whether it refers to the means of transporting goods and persons or to flows of commodities, capital, and money, or electronic information transfer and information processing, or the circulatory process between humanity, technology, and nature. Timelines show globalization tendencies running in many dimensions. The term is just as applicable to the intercontinental dissemination of telecommunications, mass tourism, or mass culture as it is to the border-crossing risks of high technology and arms trafficking, the global side-effects of overburdened ecosystems, or the supranational collective network of governmental or non-governmental organizations.[9]

But the most significant dimension is economic globalization, whose new quality can hardly be doubted: "Global economic transactions, if measured against nationally limited economic activity, are reaching a level achieved in no other previous epoch, and directly affect national economies on a previously unknown scale."[10] Here I will mention four facts. The expansion and intensification of trade in industrial goods between nations is documentable not just for the last few decades, but also in comparison with the free-trade period prior to 1914. Further, there is general agreement on the rapidly rising amount and increasing influence of transnational corporations with worldwide production facilities, and the increase in direct foreign investments. Finally, there is no doubt concerning the unparalleled acceleration of capital flows through the electronic networks of global financial markets, and the growing autonomy of financial circulatory processes, which assume a dynamic of their own distinct from the real economy. These developments culminate in considerably heightened international competition. Twenty years ago, forward-looking economists had already foreseen a "global" economy diverging from the more familiar forms of an "international" economy: "The international economy had been the object of the regulatory systems built up nationally and internationally in the postwar years. The global economy was a very largely unregulated (and many would argue unregulatable) domain. The global economy was the matrix of 'globalization' as a late twentieth century phenomenon."[11]

In themselves, these trends still don't imply any damage to the conditions for a functional and legitimate democratic process as such. But they do signal a danger for the nation-state as its institutional form. In contrast to the territorial form of the nation-state, "globalization" conjures up images of overflowing rivers, washing away all the frontier checkpoints and controls, and ultimately the bulwark of the nation itself.[12] The new relevance of "flow volumes" also signals how the locus of control has shifted from space to time: as "masters of speed" come to replace "rulers of territory," the nation-state appears to steadily lose its power.[13] State borders are certainly not comparable with fortifications – despite neurotic surveillance by national defense forces. The example of traditional foreign trade policies is enough to show that national borders actually function as internally operated "floodgates," meant to regulate the currents so that only the desired influxes (or outflows) are permitted. To see whether (and if applicable which) various features of globalization actually weaken the capacity of the nation-state to maintain its borders and to autonomously regulate exchange processes with its external environment, we will need to examine these features one by one.

Which aspects of globalization could potentially degrade the capacity for democratic self-steering within a national society? Are there functional equivalents at the supranational level for deficits that emerge at the level of the nation-state? The fear expressed by questions such as these is obvious: "Is economic globalization an uncontrollable, inflexible force to which liberal democracy is inevitably subordinate?"[14] If we proceed once again through the conditions for a functional and legitimate welfare-state mass democracy as described in (a) through (d) above, we will find a differentiated set of responses to this question, spanning the processes of globalization in their full range, without limiting ourselves to the transformation of the international economic system, central though such a transformation is.

II

How does globalization affect (a) the security of the rule of law and the effectiveness of the administrative state, (b) the sovereignty of the territorial state, (c) collective identity, and (d) the democratic legitimacy of the nation-state?[15]

(a) The first question is one of the continued effectiveness of public administration as the medium for democratic societies to intervene effectively in their own course. The total proportion of gross domestic product available for state consumption determines a very different relation between public and private sectors in Sweden, for example, than in the United States. Yet regardless of what portion of total resources the state consumes, state and society remain functionally separate from each other. Unlike regulatory functions that the state has assumed for the goals of macroeconomic steering and redistribution, there is no trace of a waning power of the nation-state for more classical organizational functions, above all for state guarantees of property rights and conditions for fair competition.

Ecological degradation and unreliable high-tech facilities have generated new kinds of risk that do not respect national borders. "Chernobyl," "ozone hole," "acid rain" are accidents and ecological changes whose scope and severity render them unmanageable from within a national framework; in this sense they overwhelm the capacities of individual states to maintain internal order.[16] State borders are growing increasingly porous in other respects as well. One need only think of organized crime, above all of international trafficking in drugs and arms. Election strategies often overdramatize the issue of domestic security, but the electorate appears very receptive to populist incitements of this sort. Nevertheless, we have also seen that the power of political control that the nation-state is steadily losing can be compensated for at the international level. Global environmental consortia perhaps do not operate with as much effectiveness as could be wished for, but they certainly do make a difference.

Things are different when we look at the capacity of the tax-based state to extract the national resources that the administration depends on for its survival. Increased capital mobility makes the state's access to profits and monetary wealth more difficult, and heightened local competition reduces the state's capacity to collect taxes. The mere threat of capital flight touches off a tax-cutting spiral (and hinders national tax enforcement agencies from imposing valid laws). Taxation at the highest income brackets, capital gains taxes, and corporate taxes have fallen to such a low level in the OECD countries that the proportion of total tax revenues derived from corporate profits has drastically fallen since the end of the 1980s, meaning that the proportion derived from excise taxes and tax on regular wage earners has seen a corresponding rise. The slogan describing a "slimmed-down state" is due less to justified criticisms of an immovable bureaucracy that new managerial skills are supposed to take on[17] and far more to the fiscal pressure that globalization is exerting on the tax-based resources of the state.

(b) As we consider the "disempowerment" of the nation-state, we think in the first instance of the long-established transformations of the modern state that first emerged with the Peace of Westphalia. The features of this system are reflected in the requirements of classical international law just as much as in the descriptions of realist political scientists.[18] According to this model, the world of states consists of nation-states regarded as independent actors within an anarchic environment, who make more or less rational decisions in pursuit of the preservation and expansion of their own power. This picture changes very little if states are seen as economic utility maximizers instead of accumulators of political power. Picturing them in economic terms may make cooperative strategies fit somewhat better into this model,[19] but the presupposition of strategic interactions among independently operating powers remains. This conventional model is less and less appropriate to the current situation.[20]

While the state's sovereignty and monopoly on violence remain formally intact, the growing interdependencies of a world society challenge the basic premise that national politics, circumscribed within a determinate national territory, is still adequate to address the actual fates of individual nation-states.

We can see this easily enough with the standard example of a nuclear reactor that a neighboring country has built near a common border, and which does not meet the planning and safety standards of one's own country. In an increasingly economically, culturally, and ecologically interconnected world, it is increasingly rare that the legitimate decisions made by states harmonize with the interests of the persons and areas potentially affected by these decisions in the state's social and territorial surroundings. Because nation-states must make decisions on a territorial basis, in an interdependent world society there is less and less congruence between the group of participants in a collective decision and the total of all those affected by their decision.[21] Theory-formation must avoid the "territorial trap": "The territorial state has been 'prior to' and 'a container' of society only under specific conditions."[22] Other borders, which are just as important for national interests as the nation-state's borders themselves, emerge with the formation of military blocs, or through economic networks – through NATO, or the OECD, or the so-called Triad – beyond the borders of the nation-state.

On the regional, international and global levels, "regimes" have emerged that make "governance beyond the nation-state" (Michael Zürn) possible, and at least partially compensate for the nation-state's lost capacities in some functional spheres.[23] This is the case in the economic sphere with the International Monetary Fund and the World Bank (1944) or the World Trade Organization that emerged from the GATT treaty (1948), as well as in other areas such as the World Health Organization (1946), the International Nuclear Regulatory Agency (1957), or the "special agencies" of the UN, for example the worldwide coordination of civil aviation. The practices of a decentralized, multi-level politics, running alongside or below the level of the UN, can at least in some respects close the efficiency gaps that open up as the nation-state loses its autonomy – even if, as remains unproven, such politics cannot really help much in the truly relevant goal of a positive coordination of social and economic policies. But loose international arrangements such as the G-7 summits, or increasingly interconnected regimes like NAFTA or ASEAN, or indeed the basic political structures of the European Union, are enough to show why the fundamental distinction between foreign and domestic policy is growing increasingly blurry for nation-states; and why, for example, diplomacy in the classical sense increasingly overlaps with cultural or foreign trade policies. Clearly, the application of "soft power" is an even more effective check against the exercise of classic political power than the normative constraints of the rules and regulations of the UN.

Naturally, legitimation gaps also open up as competencies and jurisdictions are shifted from the national to the supranational level. Alongside a number of international governmental organizations and standing conferences, non-governmental organizations such as the World Wide Fund For Nature, Greenpeace, or Amnesty International have also gained a good deal of influence, and are engaged in an informal regulatory network in a variety of ways. But these new forms of international cooperation lack the degree of legitimation even remotely approaching the requirements for procedures institutionalized via nation-states.[24]

(c) The problem of democratic deficits doesn't just arise for intergovernmental regulations, which are based on agreements between collective actors and which in any event cannot have the legitimating force of a politically constituted civil society. Beyond this, there is the further question of whether globalization also affects the cultural substrate of civil solidarity that developed in the context of the nation-state. Regarded as the institutionalized capacity for democratic self-determination, the political integration of citizens into a large-scale society counts among the undisputed historical achievements of the nation-state. But today signs of political fragmentation betray the first breaches in this façade of "the nation."

Here I am not referring primarily to nationalist conflicts such as those in the Basque regions of Spain, or in Northern Ireland. Nothing of the seriousness and gravity of these conflicts is lost if one sees them as the delayed consequences of a history of nation-building that has generated historical fault lines. Looked at normatively, this purported "right" to national self-determination, which underlay the new European order following the First World War – and which is responsible for an enormous amount of havoc – is sheer nonsense. Of course, acts of secession are often historically justified, as in cases of colonial domination, or aboriginal peoples who have been assimilated within a state without their consent. But in general, demands for "national independence" are legitimate only as a response to the repression of minorities whom the central government has deprived of equal rights, specifically rights to cultural equality.[25] Nor am I thinking here of ethnonational conflicts, such as the ones in the former Yugoslavia, which break out as an old order of political domination collapses. Local explanations suffice for cases such as these; for a range of other phenomena, however, global causes are at work.

Our own prosperous societies are witnessing a rise of ethnocentric reactions against anything foreign – hatred and violence against foreigners, against other faiths and races; also against marginalized groups, the handicapped and – once again – Jews. The loss of solidarity touched off by issues of redistribution can lead to political fragmentation, as is shown by the Northern League's efforts to separate the prosperous north of Italy from the rest of the country, or here in Germany by the calls for a revision of the financial agreements aimed at eliminating the economic disparities between the different federal states, as well as the resolution passed at the national convention of the Free Democratic Party to dismantle the so-called "solidarity supplement."*

We need to distinguish between two different aspects here: on the one hand, the cognitive dissonances that lead to a hardening of national identities as different cultural forms of life come into collision; on the other hand, the hybrid differentiations that soften native cultures and comparatively homogen-

---

* Special tax increment earmarked for economic development in the former East Germany. *Ed.*

ous forms of life in the wake of assimilation into a single material world culture.

(c-1) The woes of political oppression, civil war, and poverty no longer remain merely local affairs, if only because the media see to it that the prosperity gaps between North and South, West and East are perceived worldwide. And while this media coverage may not cause the flow of migration, it certainly accelerates it. Even if the majority of emigrants never even reach the borders of OECD societies, these countries have already witnessed a considerable change in the ethnic, religious, and cultural composition of their populations, through migrations desired, migrations tolerated, or migrations unsuccessfully resisted. Nor is it just traditional immigration countries such as the United States or the old colonial nations like Britain or France that are affected by patterns of migration. Despite harsh regulations on immigration arrayed as a protective cordon around Fortress Europe (in violation of basic constitutional rights, in the case of the Federal Republic of Germany), all European nations now find themselves on the path toward a multicultural society. Naturally, this pluralization of life forms will not be without frictions.[26] On one side, the democratic constitutional state is better equipped than other political forms to handle this pluralization; on the other side, the problems arising from immigration and pluralization of life forms pose a real challenge for nation-states in the classical mold.[27]

From a normative point of view, the fact that the democratic process must always be embedded in a common political culture doesn't imply the exclusivist project of realizing national particularity, but rather has the inclusive meaning of a practice of self-legislation that includes all citizens equally.[28] Inclusion means that a collective political existence keeps itself open for the inclusion of citizens of every background, without enclosing these others into the uniformity of a homogenous community. A previous background consensus, constructed on the basis of cultural homogeneity and understood as a necessary catalyzing condition for democracy, becomes superfluous to the extent that public, discursively structured processes of opinion- and will-formation make a reasonable political understanding possible, even among strangers. Thanks to its procedural properties, the democratic process has its own mechanisms for securing legitimacy; it can, when necessary, fill the gaps that open in social integration, and can respond to the changed cultural composition of a population by generating a common political culture.

At the same time, however, it is also true that the national basis for civic solidarity has become second nature, and this national foundation is shaken by the policies and regulations that are required for the construction of a "multicultural civil society."[29] Multicultural societies require a "politics of recognition" because the identity of each individual citizen is woven together with collective identities, and must be stabilized in a network of mutual recognition. The individual's existential dependence on intersubjectively shared traditions and identity-forming communities explains why the integrity of the legal person cannot be secured without equal cultural rights in culturally differentiated societies: "The individual's right to culture stems from the fact that every person has an overriding interest in his personal identity – that is in preserving his way of life and in preserving traits that are central identity components for him and other members of his cultural group."[30]

For nation-states with their own national histories, a politics that seeks the coexistence of different ethnic communities, language groups, religious faiths, etc. under equal rights naturally entails a process as precarious as it is painful. The majority culture, supposing itself to be identical with the national culture as such, has to free itself from its historical identification with a *general* political culture, if all citizens are to be able to identify on equal terms with the political culture of their own country. To the degree that this decoupling of political culture from majority culture succeeds, the solidarity of citizens is shifted onto the more abstract foundation of a "constitutional patriotism."[31] If it fails, then the collective collapses into subcultures that seal themselves off from one another. But in either case it has the effect of undermining the substantial commonalities of the nation understood as a community of shared descent.

(c-2) Globalization taxes the cohesive strength of national communities in another way as well. Global markets, mass

consumption, mass communication, and mass tourism dissemi-
nate the standardized products of a mass culture (overwhel-
mingly shaped by the United States). The same consumer goods
and fashions, the same films, television programs, and best-
selling music and books spread across the globe; the same fashions in pop, techno, or jeans seize and shape the mentalities of
young people in even the most far-flung places; the same language, English assimilated in a variety of ways, serves as a
medium for understanding between the most radically different
dialects. The clocks of Western civilization keep the tempo for
the compulsory simultaneity of the nonsimultaneous. This
commodified, homogenous culture doesn't just impose itself
on distant lands, of course; in the West too, it levels out even
the strongest national differences, and weakens even the strongest local traditions. At the same time, however, new anthropological research is discovering a remarkable dialectic between
leveling and creative differentiations.[32]

For too long anthropology occupied itself with nostalgic gazing at indigenous cultures which were supposedly uprooted and
robbed of their authenticity under the pressure of commercial
homogenization. More recently, however, anthropology has
come to concentrate on the constructive impulses and the
multitude of innovative responses that the lure of the global
has provoked in local contexts. Reacting to the homogenizing
pressure of a material world culture, new constellations often
emerge which do not so much level out existing cultural differences as create a new multiplicity of hybridized forms. This
observation is just as true for cities such as Moscow or London
as it is for Cameroon, Trinidad, or Belize, or for Egyptian or
Australian villages.[33] A study of the densely populated, eth-
nically mixed suburbs of West London, in the vicinity of Hea-
throw Airport, confirms the emergence of *new* cultural
differences.[34] In this context, the author of the study attacks
the hardened fiction that ethnic groups make up coherent
totalities with clearly delimited cultures. Against traditional
images of multicultural dialogue, he proposes the dynamic
image of an ongoing construction of new modes of belonging,
new subcultures and lifestyles, a process kept in motion
through intercultural contacts and multiethnic connections.

This strengthens a trend toward individualization and the emergence of "cosmopolitan identities," already evident in postindustrial societies.[35]

The tendency of supposedly homogenous subcultures to seal themselves off from one another may be due in part to attempts to reappropriate real communities, or to invent imaginary ones. One way or another, this tendency is related to the constructive differentiation of new collective forms of life, and new individual life projects. Both tendencies strengthen centrifugal forces within the nation-state, and will sap the resources of civil solidarity unless the historical symbiosis of republicanism and nationalism can be broken, and the republican sensibilities of populations can be shifted onto the foundation of constitutional patriotism.[36]

(d) A democratic order does not inherently need to be mentally rooted in "the nation" as a pre-political community of shared destiny. The strength of the democratic constitutional state lies precisely in its ability to close the holes of social integration through the political participation of its citizens. Once embedded within a liberal political culture, the democratic process itself can then guarantee a sort of emergency backup system for maintaining the integrity of a functionally differentiated society, in cases where the multiplicity of interests, cultural forms of life, or worldviews overwhelms the supposedly natural substrate of a community of shared descent.[37] In complex societies, it is the deliberative opinion- and will-formation of citizens, grounded in the principles of popular sovereignty, that forms the ultimate medium for a form of abstract, legally constructed solidarity that reproduces itself through political participation. Certainly, the democratic process has to be stabilized through its results for it to have any hopes of securing the solidarity of citizens against the internal forces that threaten to blow a society apart. And the democratic process can defuse the danger of a collapse of solidarity only if it fulfills recognized standards of social justice.

Basic human rights, and rights to political participation, constitute a self-referential model of citizenship, insofar as they enable democratically united citizens to shape their own status legislatively. Taking the long view, the only kind of democratic process that will count as legitimate, and that will be able to provide its citizens with solidarity, will be one that succeeds in an appropriate allocation and a fair distribution of rights. But to remain a source of solidarity, the status of citizenship has to maintain a use-value: it has to *pay* to be a citizen, in the currency of social, ecological, and cultural rights as well. In this sense, the policy initiatives of the social state have now assumed a considerable legitimizing function. This isn't just relevant for the core function of the social welfare state – the implementation of redistributive social policies, which are matters of existential importance for the lives of its citizens. Beyond redistributive policies, "social policy" in the broadest sense – labor policies and youth policies, health care, family, and educational policies, environmental protection and urban planning – covers the whole spectrum of the state's services that produce collective goods and secure the social, natural, and cultural living conditions that protect urbanity, the public space of a civilized society as such, from collapse. The infrastructures of public and private life are indeed threatened with collapse, destruction, or devaluation if they are given over to the regulatory powers of the market. But when I use the term "social welfare state" [*Sozialstaat*] in what follows, I am thinking less of these regulatory accomplishments in the areas of social policy, and more of the state's core function of redistribution.

Economic globalization obviously has an impact on the shrinking tax base that the state uses to finance its social policies. Even if there can be no serious talk of "dismantling" the social welfare state in the Federal Republic of Germany, as there is in Britain and the United States, there has been a demonstrable reduction of social budgets for OECD countries generally since the mid-1970s, at the same time as states have made access to their social security systems much tighter. Further, the end of Keynesian economic policy is no less significant than the crisis of public budgets. Under the pressure of globalizing markets, national governments steadily lose their capacity to influence economic cycles.[38] The interplay between social and economic policies on the one side, and between economic policy and the development of the labor market on the other, demonstrates how little room remains for the effective exercise of legitimized domestic policy.

In the postwar era, the Bretton Woods system of fixed exchange rates, together with the institutions of the World Bank and the IMF, helped to create an international economic regime that struck a balance between national economic policies and the rules of liberalized global trade. After this system was abandoned in the early 1970s, an entirely different system of "transnational liberalism" emerged. Since then global markets have progressively liberalized, capital mobility has accelerated, and industrial mass production has shifted to meet the needs of "post-Fordist flexibility."[39] Increasingly globalized markets have clearly worked to the disadvantage of the state's autonomy and its capacity for economic interventions.[40] At the same time, multinational corporations have emerged as powerful competitors to nation-states. This shift of power is better grasped with the concepts of a theory of different steering media than with a theory of power: money replaces power. The regulatory power of collectively binding decisions operates according to a different logic than the regulatory mechanisms of the market. Power can be democratized; money cannot. Thus the possibilities for a democratic self-steering of society slip away as the regulation of social spheres is transferred from one medium to another.

Under the conditions of a globalized "locational competition,"* businesses see themselves required to raise labor productivity more and more, and to increasingly rationalize labor processes, which in turn exacerbates the long-term trend toward a reduction of the labor force. Mass layoffs are a sign of the growing threat of moveable businesses, as opposed to the generally weak position of labor unions, which normally remain tied to a specific location. In this situation, where a vicious circle of growing unemployment, overburdened social security systems, and a shrinking tax base exhausts the financial capacities of the state, growth-stimulating measures become both

---

* *Standortskonkurrenz*, which results when nation-states understand economic globalization as the challenge to increase their own economic competitiveness relative to other states, as opposed to positive modes of economic and political integration. *Ed.*

far more important and far less possible. International stock exchanges have taken over the "valuation" of national economic policies. This is also why [supply-side] policies for controlling demand consistently have counterproductive external effects on national economic cycles. "Keynesianism in one country" is no longer a possibility.[41]

As markets drive out politics, the nation-state increasingly loses its capacities to raise taxes and stimulate growth, and with them the ability to secure the essential foundations of its own legitimacy. No functional equivalents for these capacities are emerging on the supranational level. The success of the GATT negotiations certainly shows that governments can reach agreements on dismantling trade barriers and creating new markets. But so far, the only positive integration that roughly corresponds to this negative one are more or less encouraging efforts in ecological concerns. There has not even been an agreement on the so-called Tobin Tax, let alone any wide-ranging, market-correcting agreements on a coordinated tax policy, social policies, or economic programs. And despite all this, national governments, terrified of the implicit threat of capital flight, have let themselves be dragged into a cost-cutting deregulatory frenzy, generating obscene profits and drastic income disparities, rising unemployment, and the social marginalization of a growing population of the poor.[42]

To the degree that the social presuppositions for broad-based political participation are destroyed, even formally correct democratic decisions come to lose their credibility. "In order to remain competitive in ever-growing global markets, [the OECD countries] must take steps that cause irreparable harm to the cohesion of civil society . . . The most pressing task for the First World in the coming decade will thus be squaring the circle of prosperity, social cohesion, and political freedom."[43] This (not exactly encouraging) diagnosis has led politicians to scrap social programs, and has driven voters to apathy or protest. The broad renunciation of the power of politics to shape social relations, and the readiness to abandon normative points of view in favor of adaptations to supposedly unavoidable systemic imperatives, now dominate the political arenas of the Western world. Clinton or Blair, relying on empty formulas such as "It's time for a change," pitch themselves as efficient managers for the reorganization of failing business ventures. The truly programmatic vacuity of a political platform that has been whittled down to "political change" corresponds, on the side of voters, either to informed abstinence or the thirst for "political charisma," even without shady characters such as Ross Perot or Berlusconi, who come out of nowhere promoting business-style success. If the desperation is great enough, a little money is all that is needed for right-wing slogans and a remote-controlled engineer from Bitterfeld, a complete political unknown with nothing more than a cellphone at his disposal, to mobilize nearly 13 percent of the protest vote.*

III

If our analysis so far is correct, the fears of the disempowering effects of globalization are, if still vague, far from unjustified. The fiscal basis for social policies has steadily dwindled, while the state has increasingly lost its capacity to steer the economy via macroeconomic policy. Moreover, the integrational force of nationality as a way of life is diminishing, along with the relatively homogenous basis of civil solidarity. As nation-states increasingly lose both their capacities for action and the stability of their collective identities, they will find it more and more difficult to meet the need for self-legitimation. How should we react to all this?

The image of territorial masters losing control of their own borders has elicited mutually opposed rhetorical strategies, both nourished by the classical doctrine of the state. On the one side, a defensive rhetoric – used by the Federal Minister of the Interior, let's say – arises from an understanding of the state's protective function, a part of its traditional monopoly of legitimate violence: the state maintains law and order within

---

* The reference is to the surprisingly strong performance of the far-right Deutsche Volkspartei in the state parliamentary elections in Saxony-Anhalt in early 1998, in which the politically unknown party leader controlled his party officers from his seat in Bavaria. *Ed.*

the borders of its own territory and guarantees security for citizens within their own private spheres of life. This defensive rhetoric invokes the political will to close the floodgates against uncontrolled waves breaking in from the outside. The protectionist affect here is directed just as much at arms merchants and drug traffickers who threaten internal security as it is against the incoming floods of information, foreign capital, or labor immigration, or the waves of refugees who supposedly destroy native culture and standards of living. On the other side, an offensive rhetoric attacks the repressive features of the sovereign state, which consigns its citizens to the homogenizing pressure of a regulation-crazy bureaucracy, and locks them into the prison of a uniform lifestyle. Here, the libertarian affect welcomes the opening of geographical and social borders as an emancipation in two senses – as a liberation of the oppressed from the normalizing violence of state regulation, and also as the emancipation of the individual from compulsory assimilation to the behavioral patterns of the collective.[44]

Neither of these positions, neither the uncritical welcome of the globalization process nor its uncritical demonization, goes far enough, of course. Under the changed conditions of the postnational constellation, the nation-state is not going to regain its old strength by retreating into its shell. Neo-nationalist protectionism cannot explain how a world society is supposed to be divided back up into pieces, unless through a global politics which, right or wrong, it insists is a chimera. A politics of self-liquidation – letting the state simply merge into postnational networks – is just as unconvincing. And postmodern neoliberalism cannot explain how the deficits in steering competencies and legitimation that emerge at the national level can be compensated at the supranational level without new forms of political regulation. The successful use of political power has to be measured by criteria other than economic ones: money can't simply replace power. Instead, the foregoing analysis suggests the transnational task of bringing global economic networks under political control, as an alternative to futile adaptations to the imperatives of locational competition.[45] This project, of course, has to remain true to the subtle dynamic of the opening, and the renewed closure, of socially integrated lifeworlds.

Moreover, it is a project that nation-states, paradoxically, can pursue from within their current scope of possibilities, but which they could realize only beyond these current limits.

Familial bonds, religious communities, urban municipalities, empires, or states can all open and close themselves in relation to their environments. This dynamic transforms the horizon of the lifeworld, the fabric of social integration, the spheres of differentiated forms of life, and individual life projects. The relative hardness or permeability of boundaries itself doesn't reveal much about the openness or closedness of a given community. What is interesting is not so much the consistency of boundaries as the interaction between two modes for the coordination of social action: "networks" and "lifeworlds."[46] Horizontal relations of exchange and interaction, which are constructed through the market decisions of independent actors, are often stabilized through efficiently generated, positively valuated action consequences. This form of "functional integration" of social relations via networks competes with an entirely distinct form of integration – with a "social integration" of the collective lifeworld of those who share a collective identity; a social integration based on mutual understanding, intersubjectively shared norms, and collective values.

European history since the Middle Ages has been marked by the specific process of mutual encounter between these two forms of integration, with a characteristic result of opening- and closure-effects. The spread of exchange networks for commodities, money, persons, and information demands an explosive degree of mobility. The spatial and temporal horizons of a lifeworld, on the other hand, no matter how broadly they extend, always form a whole that is both intuitively present but always withdrawn to an unproblematic background; a whole which is closed in the sense that it contains every possible interaction from the perspective of lifeworld participants. Expanding and intensifying markets or communication networks ignite a modernization dynamic of opening and closure. The proliferation of anonymous relations with "others" and the dissonant experiences with "foreigners" have a subversive power. Growing pluralism loosens ascriptive ties to family, locality, social background, and tradition, and initiates a formal transformation of social integration. With each new impulse toward modernization, intersubjectively shared lifeworlds open, so that they can reorganize, and then close once more.

Circling around this formal transformation, classical sociology came up with ever new descriptions of it: from status to contract; from primary to secondary groups; from community to society; from mechanical to organic solidarity; and so on. The impulse toward opening is generated by new markets, new means of communication, new modes of commerce and cultural networks. For those affected by it, "opening" entails the ambivalent experience of increasing contingency: the disintegration of formative and hitherto authoritarian forms of dependencies; the liberation from relationships that are as orienting and protective as they are prejudicial and imprisoning. In a word, the opening of a strongly integrated lifeworld releases individuals into the ambivalence of expanded options. It opens their eyes to new possibilities, but also increases their risk of making mistakes – which will then, at least, be their own mistakes, which they can learn from. Each individual is confronted with a freedom that obliges him to count on himself alone, and that isolates him from others as it compels him to take a strategic-rational view of his own interests. And yet this freedom also enables him to enter into new social ties and to creatively draft new rules for living together with others.

If this liberalizing impulse is to avoid running into sociopathology – bogging down at the phase of de-differentiation, alienation, and anomie – then the lifeworld must successfully reorganize the structures of self-consciousness, self-determination, and self-realization that have shaped the self-understanding of modernity.[47] Lifeworlds that have disintegrated under the pressure of opening have to close themselves anew – now, of course, with *expanded* horizons. And with this new closure, individuals' capacity for action is expanded in three dimensions: an increased latitude for a reflective appropriation of identity-forming traditions; for autonomy in interactions with others and in relating to the norms of collective social life; and for the individual sphere of shaping one's own life. More or less successful learning processes thus find expression in exemplary modes of life. Many modes of living vanish without a trace over the course of history; others maintain their attraction in the memories of subsequent generations. The modes of life of the European bourgeoisie are exemplary in this sense. Like the "town burghers" in the communes of the high Middle Ages and the Renaissance, the "bourgeoisie" in the liberal nation-state of the early modern period developed – along with their specific modes of oppression and exclusion – models of self-administration and participation, of freedom and tolerance, that expressed the spirit of bourgeois emancipation.

At the close of the eighteenth century, these emancipatory experiences were articulated in the ideas of popular sovereignty and human rights. Since the era of the American and French revolutions, therefore, this "closure" of a collective political life has been conditioned by an egalitarian universalism, based on the intuition of the inclusion of the other under equal rights. This is evident today in the challenges posed by "multiculturalism" and "individualization," both of which demand the end of the symbiosis between the constitutional state and "the nation" as a community of shared descent, and a renewal of a more abstract form of civil solidarity in the sense of a universalism sensitive to difference. Globalization forces the nation-state to open itself up internally to the multiplicity of foreign, or new, forms of cultural life. At the same time, globalization shrinks the scope of action for national governments, insofar as the sovereign state must also open itself externally, in relation to international regimes. If this renewed closure is to come about without sociopathological side-effects, then politics has to catch up with globalized markets, and has to do so in institutional forms that do not regress below the legitimacy conditions for democratic self-determination.

In this respect, Karl Polanyi's book *The Great Transformation* is still instructive. Published in 1944, Polanyi's study presented fascism as the expression of a failed attempt toward political closure; as a delayed reaction to the collapse of a free-trade regime that had served as the basis for a stable currency tied to the gold standard until the beginning of the twentieth century. As a historian, Polanyi wanted to show that a mode of international trade largely freed from political regulation was in no way the spontaneous product of developing markets themselves; on the contrary, the free-trade system was constructed in the nineteenth century, under the protection of the *Pax Britannica*. As an anthropologist, Polanyi was also convinced that such a deregulated economic regime had devastating long-term consequences for "the human and natural substance of society," and led, ultimately, to anomie. On the other hand, at the time the book was written, near the end of the Second World War, the horrific consequences of a totalitarian closure of an economically shattered society made clear the necessity of "withdrawing the productive factors of ground, labor, and money from the market."[48] The future of institutionalized capitalism that Polanyi sketches in his last chapter, entitled "Freedom in a Complex Society," anticipates essential features of the postwar economic order. The Bretton Woods system, which set up the framework for the more or less successful social welfare state policy that most industrial countries followed, was founded in the same year the book was published.

Since then, the balancing act of a successful political closure with the political deregulation of global markets has come to an end. A new opening, this time via financial markets, has once again transformed the international division of labor. The dynamics of the new global economy explain the renewed interest in the dynamic of the international economy that Polanyi explored.[49] That is, if a "double movement" – the deregulation of world trade in the nineteenth century, and its re-regulation in the twentieth – can serve as a model, then we may once again be standing on the brink of a "great transformation." Polanyi's perspective, in any case, poses the question of how the political closure of a globally networked, highly interdependent world society would be possible without regressions – without the same sorts of world-historical tremors and catastrophes that we know from the first half of the twentieth century, and that spurred Polanyi's investigation.

To be sure, a renewed closure cannot be envisioned defensively, as a resistance to a supposedly "overwhelming" process of modernization. This would merely reintroduce the nostalgic attitudes of the losers of modernization, clinging to the utopian image of a "redeemed" form of life as a way of warding off despair. What turns these romantic, often peculiarly touching, fantasies into "utopian" images in the worst sense are the regressive features of an "ethical life" projected into the distance, which do justice neither to the emancipatory potential that accompanies the forced opening of a dissolving social formation, nor to the complexity of new circumstances. Not even intellectuals as dedicated to modernity as Hegel and Marx were entirely free of fantasies of this kind. At decisive points (*Philosophy of Right*, paras. 249ff), Hegel borrowed the corporatist features of the stratified guild-based societies of the early modern period to describe the ethical life of the rational state – the corporation, that is, as "second family." And the young, still not entirely unsentimental Marx fleshed out the idea of a free association of producers with memories of the corporative, communal world of peasants and craftspeople, a world that was already collapsing under the pressure of a competitive society in Marx's own time. Of course, Marx immediately turned against the early form of socialism that remained fixed on the task of "sublating" the solidary communities of a romanticized past. The dwindling reservoir of traditional forces of social integration was supposed to be transformed, and rescued, under the new labor conditions of early industrialization. Socialism too bore a Janus face over the course of the workers' movements, a face that looked back at an idealized past at the same time as it gazed into a distant future dominated by industrial labor.[50]

The industrial society of the postwar years, pacified by the social state, can't be idealized any more than pre- or early-industrial societies can. What Polanyi saw as the future of a socially domesticated capitalism at the end of the Second World War can now be described retrospectively as an "organized" or "first" modernity, which was followed after the postwar era by a "second" or "liberally expanded" modernity. This reading does avoid a particular sort of nostalgia:

> In view of the scale and the organizational form of human practices...one can speak of a relative closure of modernity...The achievements of organized modernity consisted in effecting a transition from the upheavals and uncertainties of the late nineteenth century to a new coherence of practices and institutions. Nation, class, and state were the most significant

conceptual components of this construction, which served as the basis for collective identities.[51]

According to this view, the deployment of neo-corporative negotiating systems and regulated industrial relations, mass political parties with social-structural anchoring, reliably functioning social security systems, nuclear families with inherited sexual division of labor, normalized labor relations with standardized career paths, all formed the collective background for a more or less stable society based on mass production and mass consumption.[52]

Against this background, the trends toward the de-bureaucratization of public services, the de-hierarchicalization of professional organizational forms, the de-traditionalization of familial and gender relations and the de-conventionalization of consumer patterns and lifestyles could all appear in a more favorable light. The increasing differentiation among forms of interaction and mentalities, the reliable party affiliations of voters, the new influence of subpolitical movements on organized politics, and most importantly the growing autonomization and individualization of the choice of life projects, all grant a certain charm to the relentless processes of dissolution that characterize organized modernity.[53] But these positive aspects all have their flipside: the "flexibilization" of career paths hides a deregulated labor market and a heightened risk of unemployment; the "individualization" of life projects conceals a sort of compulsory mobility that is hard to reconcile with durable personal bonds; the "pluralization" of life forms also reflects the danger of a fragmented society and the loss of social cohesion.[54] Although we should take care not to assume an uncritical view of the achievements of the social welfare state, we must also not blind ourselves to the costs of its "transformation" or collapse. One can remain sensitive to the normalizing force of social bureaucracies without closing one's eyes to the shocking price that a reckless monetarization of the lifeworld would demand.

There is no cause for naively celebrating the opening of organized modernity. For the linear narrative forms of postmodern theories, there is no further, renewed political closure to follow this opening: the capacity for collectively binding decisions, politics as such, vanishes with the collapse of the nation-state. And with its collapse, a social politics reduced to the mere "administration of the social" supposedly loses its basis. If "the responsibilities and duties of individuals are (no longer) able to be related to a delimited political order...then the possibility of politics itself is called into question."[55] For postmodernism, the new fluidity of societies after the end of the organizational form of the nation-state signals an "end of politics" – an end that neoliberalism, which wants markets to take over as many steering functions as possible, is counting on.[56] While the postmodernists are convinced that the fading of the classical world of states and the rise of an anarchically interconnected world society make politics on a global scale impossible, neoliberals see global politics as an undesirable political framework for a deregulated world economy. For different reasons, postmodernism and neoliberalism thus ultimately share the vision of the lifeworlds of individuals and small groups scattering, like discrete monads, across global, functionally coordinated networks, rather than overlapping in the course of social integration, in larger, multidimensional political entities.

We should be just as cautious with these progressivist visions of opening as with the regressive utopias of closure. Far more important is a sensitivity to the particular balance between opening and closure, a balance that has been characteristic of the happier periods of European modernization. We will only be able to meet the challenges of globalization in a reasonable manner if the postnational constellation can successfully develop new forms for the democratic self-steering of society. Therefore I would like to test the conditions for a democratic politics beyond the nation-state through the exemplary case of the European Union. Here I am interested less in the motives for or against the further development of the political union, and more in the strength of the reasons that can engage both supporters and skeptics; reasons for and against the gamble on a postnational democracy. There are additional reasons in favor of European unification that have nothing to do with the question of how democracy can survive the nation-state as the form of its realization. For many of us, the historical background plays a role that makes a currency union – and the incorporation of Germany into a European community – irreversible. In what follows, however, the question is limited to the reasons for and against the European Union as the initial form for a postnational democracy.[57]

IV

I will begin by distinguishing between four positions on this question, according to the degree of support for a postnational democracy: Euroskeptics, Market Europeans, Eurofederalists, and proponents of "global governance." Euroskeptics see the introduction of the euro as a fundamental mistake, or at least as premature. Market Europeans grudgingly accept the unified currency as a necessary consequence of the end of domestic markets, but do not want to go any further than that. Eurofederalists work toward transforming existing international treaties into a political constitution, in order to build a basis of legitimacy for the supranational decisions of commissions, ministerial councils, the European Court of Justice, and the European Parliament. Last come the representatives of the cosmopolitan alternative, who regard a Federal States of Europe as the initial basis for constructing the regime for a future "world domestic policy," to be secured through international treaties. These four positions are the consequence of responses to a series of already established questions, and I will thus take up four of these questions that are decisive for framing the terms of the current debate.

First (a) is the thesis of the end of the labor-based society. If within the framework of normal labor relations, employment loses its formative power to structure society at large, then the recreation of a "full employment society" is no longer plausible as a political goal. But wide-ranging reforms of the employment system cannot be expected to succeed within the limits of national borders; they would require a coordinated effort through agreements and procedures on the supranational level. The question of the European Union also begins a new round in the old battle (b) between social justice and market efficiency. Neoliberals are convinced that global markets can both make economies more efficient and meet demands for redistributive justice; otherwise the option favored by Market Europeans, a loose union of existing nation-states integrated horizontally via a unified market, would lose all its plausibility. Third (c) is the question of whether the European Union can even begin to compensate for the lost competencies of the nation-state. As a test case, I will look at aspects of redistributive social policies. This question of the competence to act depends on another, analytically distinct question, (d): whether political communities form a collective identity beyond national borders, and thus whether they can meet the legitimacy conditions for a postnational democracy. If these two last questions can't be answered affirmatively, then a Federal States of Europe is ruled out, and with it the basis for any broader hopes.

The key terms that I use here can at best only help to characterize a discourse whose outcome cannot be predicted, and to assign a certain division of the burdens of proof. Only in this connection could one judge a "cosmopolitan" position, which calls for a renewed political closure of an economically unmastered world society.

(a) The trend toward increased productivity, which we can observe in all industrial societies, has continued in postindustrial societies as well; ongoing rationalization of production processes is normally accompanied by a significant shift of the working population from the primary to the secondary and tertiary sectors, and finally to the quarternary sector of a knowledge- and information-based society. Repeated prognoses of "technological unemployment" resulting from this shift have not been confirmed, at least not in its early phases. Until well into the 1970s, through all economic ups and downs, job losses were compensated by a combination of job creation and a shorter working week. Since then we have witnessed a decoupling of economic growth and unemployment rates in most OECD countries. Current unemployment figures – 18 million according to official EU statistics – are the product of a situation in which every economic upturn has left a higher base level of unemployment in its wake. Other countries, like the United States and Great Britain, have created low-wage sectors that have more fully met demands for basic services. But this has also had an effect on the dynamic of impoverishment and marginalization, which has been shifted from the level of society to that of the individual: a higher degree of state repression and the undermining of the public standards of social solidarity.

Various causes are adduced for the phenomenon of growing social inequities; most significantly the end of Keynesian economic policies and heightened global competition, which increases investments in the rationalization and modernization of production. Paul Kennedy has calculated the magnitude of a reserve labor force that mobile capital will create in Asia, Latin America, and other countries in the coming decades. Of course, many other causes of social inequity cannot be brought into any simple causal relation with globalization. In most OECD countries, the size of the workforce in absolute terms has risen due to the growing number of women entering into employment, as well as increased numbers of immigrants, economic refugees, and so on. Because existential need is at issue here, labor markets cannot regulate the surplus labor force according to the usual mechanisms of supply and demand that they would use for markets in goods – this too is a part of the special character of "the commodity of labor power." Moreover, local conditions and failed economic policies play a role: inflexible public administrations, for example, or a poorly trained workforce, or delayed structural adaptations. Finally, a lack of imagination on the part of management, poor professional organization, the failure of research and development to come up with new innovations, or an inadequate reconnection between industry and science can all detract from the relative competitiveness of national positions, with relevant consequences for employment.

How we evaluate the thesis of the "end of the full-employment society" (Voruba) obviously depends on how we weigh all these causes, and the weight will not depend on any simple choice between the Left and the Right. The Commission on the Future of the Free States of Bavaria and Saxony, headed by Meinhard Miegel, proceeded on the assumption that the Federal Republic of Germany will have to deal with permanent high unemployment levels, while at the same time the Friedrich-Ebert Foundation Commission on the Future concluded that employment, now as before, is the "key indicator of social integration," even as employment's basic character, "including the image of a stable, lifelong career," will be drastically transformed.[58] An anticipated continuity of the structures of a laboring society relieves politics of the task of radically restructuring the system of distribution. Under certain conditions it is even enough if the state simply remains active within the national context to improve the structural conditions for capital utilization.

The situation appears differently if one abandons full employment as a political goal. Under these new premises, one can either try to lower current standards of redistributive justice, as a way of dismantling a social welfare state now regarded as a "misdevelopment." Or one can look to alternatives that are themselves by no means without cost: for example, a radical redistribution of the lower volume of employment[59], or the participation of broad strata of society in capital assets[60] or decoupling a state-backed minimum income above the level of social assistance from earned income.[61] Radical redistributions of this sort will meet with resistance from existing interests, value orientations, and property relations; in a national context, they will also have little chance of being realized in a cost-neutral or competition-neutral way. During the 1970s, discussions of a minimum income and a dual economy were still based on the premise that the nation-state could carry out this social restructuring on its own. But given the transformation of global structural conditions, it is now clear that innovative answers to the "end of the labor-based society" require a coordinated approach on a supranational level.

(b) The neoliberal alternative mentioned earlier touches on the old controversy over the relation between social justice and market efficiency. I will certainly not be able to contribute anything new toward resolving this time-honored battle of dogmas. We must face the fact that a broadly deregulated labor market, and the privatization of provision for illness, old age, and unemployment, will all allow an impoverished milieu to emerge at the very edge of the minimum requirements for existence in areas with low incomes and poor employment conditions. Even if the majority of the satisfied, and the not-all-that-satisfied, could bring themselves to simply hand over the remainder of the population – a hopelessly "superfluous" population, marginalized from the political process – to a repressive state as a problem for internal security and social relief, this forced desolidarization of society would remain a thorn in the flesh of the political culture.[62] A functional justification is not enough to make egregious social differences normatively acceptable in a democratically constituted civil society. At this point, neoliberalism as a normative theory assumes the burden of proof for the strong view that efficient markets will guarantee not just an optimal relation of cost and benefit, but a just distribution of social goods as well. This raises two questions: Which normative expectations, exactly, are efficient markets supposed to fulfill? And how likely is it that markets will function so efficiently that we can expect to see a normatively acceptable distribution, even in this (as we shall see) reduced sense of social justice?

Neoliberalism's most fundamental normative assumptions rest on a conception of just exchange borrowed from the procedural model of contract law. In any act of exchange, the benefit, acquisition, or profit – what somebody receives, that is – stands in an "equivalent" relation to what he brings in – i.e. to cost, offer, or investment – only if the agreement, the consent on both sides of the exchange, is made under certain standard conditions: the participants must have equal freedom to decide according to their own preferences. A market that is institutionalized not just through the medium of money but also via equal liberal private rights, in particular property rights and the freedom to enter into contracts, secures a procedure for the exchange of equivalents. This procedure is thus "just" if and to the extent that it actually makes free competition possible, where "free" is taken in the strongly normative sense of the same personal freedom for all. In this sense, merit-based pay

counts as a special case of just exchange, which is connected
with the presumption of reciprocally assumed freedom of will.

This conception of freedom is linked with a normatively
diminished conception of the person. The concept of the person as a "rational decider" is not only independent of the idea
of the moral person who determines her will through an insight
into what is in the equal interests of all those affected; it is also
independent of the concept of the citizen of a republic, who
participates in the public practice of self-legislation under equal
rights. Neoliberal theory deals with private subjects who "do
and permit what they will" according to their own preferences
and value orientations within the limits of legally permissible
action. They are not required to take any mutual interest for
one another; they are thus not equipped with any moral sense
of social obligation. The legally requisite respect for private
liberties that all competitors are equally entitled to is something
very different from the equal respect for the human worth of
each individual.

With this concept of a "society based on private rights,"
neoliberalism also calculates that the use-value of civil liberties
is consumed in the enjoyment of private autonomy. The state
apparatus has the instrumental task of reaching collectively
binding decisions according to the criterion of the aggregated
preferences of citizens. Of course, the democratic process protects equal private liberties, but for neoliberalism it does not
add political autonomy as a further dimension of freedom.
Neoliberalism is thus unreceptive to the republican idea of
self-legislation, according to which private and civic autonomy
mutually presuppose one another. It closes itself off from the
intuition that citizens can be free only if they can regard themselves as both the authors and the addressees of the law at the
same time.

This double normative foreshortening that neoliberalism
assumes with its choice of basic concepts may explain its particular lack of concern with questions of social justice – an
attitude somewhere between toleration, indifference, and cyni-
cism which, in Germany, often comes mixed with a pessimistic
anthropology of an entirely different pedigree. Markets, of
course, if they are actually operating "efficiently," that is,

according to the assumptions of the market model, cannot fulfill even these reduced normative expectations. I don't need to go into the familiar objections in detail.[63] With good reason, markets are prized for their ability to link efficient and cost-effective information transfer with incentives for expedient information-processing. But this function is fundamentally constrained by external costs; markets are deaf to information that is not expressed in the language of price. Moreover, real markets determine prices only very incompletely, since they normally only very imperfectly approach the ideal requirements of free competition. And the equalizing force of markets, which is supposed to measure the performance of all competitors by a neutral criterion, fails due to the evident fact that persons, as we know them, simply do not have the same opportunities to participate in markets and to generate profits. Real markets reproduce, and exacerbate, existing relative advantages of businesses, households, and individuals *ex ante*.

(c) Neoliberalism's position on the desirability of deregulated markets leads to a preference for a unified European market and a common monetary policy overseen by an independent central bank. The social-democratic option, in which a state government creates a framework for efficient markets while closing the gap between market efficiency and social solidarity, on the contrary, is often associated with the attitude of Euroskepticism. Here the question of whether the European Union will be in any position to assume essential tasks of the nation-state becomes decisive. Corresponding to this question is the further question of what sort of political freedom of action national governments still retain.

Euroskeptics assume that the nation-state has provided the setting for the emergence of different configurations of non-economic practices, institutions, and mentalities, and that these have all endowed every economic position with a distinctive profile, largely determining relative prospects for success in global competition. This assumption is supported by research exploring the institutional embeddedness of national systems of production; research which has the goal of refuting the abstractions of neoclassical economic theory.[64] Obviously, in any given market constellation there is no one "right" path to the cost-effective combination of labor force, capital, and raw materials: "Social systems of production vary not only in the ways that firms approach profits, but also in the degree to which they attempt to maximize (a) criteria of allocative efficiency or X-efficiency considerations, (b) social peace and egalitarian distribution considerations, (c) quantity vs. quality aspects of production, and (d) innovation in developing new products vs. innovation in improving on existing products."[65] From this perspective, for example, the Friedrich-Ebert Foundation Commission on the Future worked up a profile of Germany's overall economic position that emphasizes the state's role in enhancing local advantages, rather than a neoliberal cost-cutting strategy.[66]

Of course, the impressive catalog of issues for a national reform policy (improving innovative capacities, developing human resources, modernizing management, creating a bearable low-wage sector with a negative income tax, etc.) does not touch on the fact that globalization, as has been discussed, both cuts into tax revenues and reduces the state's ability to implement employment policies and stimulate economic growth, bringing social policy as such into enormous trouble. Hence Euroskeptics cannot be satisfied with merely eulogizing the virtues of the dearly departed nation-state. They turn the tables, and ask whether the European Union has any real hope of regaining the political capacity for action that nation-states have forfeited according to the Eurofederalist interpretation. What remains uncontested is the heavy net of regulations that the European Commission, the Council of Ministers, and, to a considerable degree, the European Court have thrown over the societies of participating states. A policy for Europe, which from the beginning pursued the goal of the free mobility of goods and services, capital and persons, must cut across many different political fields.[67] This counts for social policy as well. For example, the European Union has enacted important social legislation regarding the equality of women, while the European Court of Justice has produced over 300 decisions relevant for social law, with the goal of making national welfare systems compatible with the common domestic market. But adaptations such as these have no bearing on the modes of taxation, financing, and distribution that are established by the socio-political systems of member countries – systems that vary greatly in design and performance levels.

If the consequences of currency union and a unified European monetary policy mean that member states become even less capable of macroeconomic steering, while competition within Europe grows even sharper, then we can expect problems of an entirely new magnitude to arise. Countries that enjoy high social standards fear the danger of a downward adjustment; countries with a comparatively weak social safety net fear that the imposition of higher standards will rob them of their cost advantages. Europe will be faced with the choice of either eliminating the pressure of these problems by consigning them to the market – in the form of competition between sociopolitical systems remaining under national jurisdiction – or meeting these problems politically, with an effort toward "harmonization" on important questions of social policy, labor policy, and tax policy. I don't need to recapitulate the details of debates amongst the experts.[68] At the heart of the matter is the question of whether European institutions, on the path toward a negative integration, are in a position to reconcile national interests to a degree sufficient to create new markets; or whether, beyond this, they are powerful enough to make mar-ket-correcting decisions for a positive integration, and can thus carry out redistributive regulations. Along with the stability of currency rates, employment and continued economic growth are equally important, ongoing economic and political goals which, if necessary, will have to be pursued in competition with an independent central bank.[69]

The skeptical side argues on the basis of the historical evid-ence of a twice-failed attempt to develop a social dimension of European politics, and to develop the European community sociopolitically into a federation.[70] Wolfgang Streek has analyzed the various coalitions and strategies that have consist-ently reduced such ambitious projects at harmonization to the market-oriented goal of eliminating the obstacles for the mobil-ity of national labor markets. The other, optimistic side, by contrast, emphasizes the self-interest, capacity for action, and relative independence of European authorities as opposed to national governments, politicians' unwillingness to deviate from policy courses once they have been laid down, or on the recalcitrance and the growing interconnectedness of the very problems that demand regulation.[71] Euro-optimists can always point out that in other areas, the European Union has pursued an active if modest redistribution policy for quite some time – a redistribution between economic sectors through a common agrarian policy, and a redistribution between regions through the use of economic development funds.

So far, the discussion seems to lead to the conclusion that neither side is right: neither the neorealists with their faith that the nation-state alone can pursue a "formative" politics, nor the neofunctionalists who wait for a kind of "automatic" development from domestic markets to a federation of states. "The future of European social policy does not depend on whether a European domestic market needs institutionalization...but whether Europe as a political system can summon the necessary political resources to impose redistributive duties on powerful participants in the market."[72] Currency union is the final step on a path that its initiators began with very high hopes; a path that today can be described much more soberly, in retrospect, as an "intergovernmental market construction." Today, we have reached the point where the thick horizontal net stretched over markets by relatively weak political regulations is now being expanded by even more weakly legitimized authorities. The dynamic of European unification can lead beyond this point only if Eurofederalists can design a future Europe in contrast to the status quo that the Market Europeans would like to see maintained; one that can stir the imagination and help to initiate a broad public debate over the common issues for different national arenas.

(d) The political alternative to the neoliberal vision of a market-based Europe can be defended against the predictable economic objections by pointing out that the European economic sphere as a whole still enjoys a relatively strong independence from global competition, due to its dense regional interconnections of trade and direct investments. But even if one grants that Europe still has some economic latitude for political action – i.e. still has the power to implement effective economic policies – transforming the European Union into a federation still depends on one further condition: "A strengthening of the governing capacities of European institutions is unthinkable without an expansion of their formal democratic basis of legitimacy."[73] If Europe is to be able to act on the basis of an integrated, multilevel policy, then European citizens, who are initially characterized as such only by their common passports, will have to learn to mutually recognize one another as members of a common political existence beyond national borders: They must not "suspect members of other European nations of 'unreasonable' harm to 'our' interests," whether measured "by intention or result."[74]

Of course, a constitution for a multinational state on the scale of the European Union cannot simply adopt the model of constitutions of national federations such as the Federal Republic of Germany.[75] It is neither possible nor desirable to level out the national identities of member nations, nor melt them down into a "Nation of Europe." To put it simply, in a European Federation the second chamber of government representatives would have to hold a stronger position than the directly elected parliament of popular representatives, because the elements of negotiations and multilateral agreements between member states that are decisive today cannot disappear without a trace even for a union under a political constitution. But positively coordinated redistribution policies must be borne by a Europe-wide democratic will-formation, and this cannot happen without a basis of solidarity. The form of civil solidarity that has been limited to the nation-state until now has to expand to include all citizens of the union, so that, for example, Swedes and Portuguese are willing to take responsibility for one another. Only then can citizens be reasonably expected to support roughly comparable minimum wages, or simply equal conditions for individual life projects, which will continue to be molded by the nation. The next steps toward a European Federation involve extraordinary risks, for one fundamental reason: expanding Europe's political capacity for action has to happen simultaneously with the expansion of the basis of legitimation of European institutions.

On the one hand, the sociopolitical damage inflicted by deregulatory competition between national "positions," overseen by a supposedly neutral central bank, can be avoided only if the common European monetary policy is expanded to include a common tax policy, social policy, and economic policy, whose cumulative effect would be strong enough to discourage individual nations from taking unilateral measures. This, in turn, would require that still more of nation-states' sovereign rights be transferred to a European government, while nation-states would essentially only maintain those regulatory competencies that would be unlikely to produce unwanted side-effects for the "internal" affairs of other member states. In other words, the European Union must be repositioned from its previous basis of international treaties, to a "Charter" in the form of a basic law. On the other hand, this transition from intergovernmental agreements to a common political existence under a constitution does not just aim for a common procedure of democratic legislation that would supersede nationally defined voting rights and national public spheres; rather it would aim toward a common practice of opinion- and will-formation, nourished by the roots of a European civil society, and expanded into a Europe-wide political arena. This condition for the legitimacy of a postnational democracy is obviously a long way from being fulfilled today. Euroskeptics doubt that it can be fulfilled at all.

Of course, the argument that there is no such thing as a European people, and thus also no force capable of generating a European constitution,[76] only becomes a fundamental objection through a particular use of the concept of "a people."[77] The prognosis that there cannot be any such thing as a European people remains plausible only if "the people," as a source of solidarity, actually depends on some corresponding community as a pre-political basis of trust, which fellow countrymen and women inherit as the shared fate of their socialization. Even Claus Offe backs up his own skeptical conclusions with the premise that the willingness of citizens to expose themselves to the risks of a redistributive social state cannot be fully explained without this ascriptive form of solidarity, the sense of being "one of us." On this reading, only a sense of national belonging understood as membership in a pre-political community of fate can exert the kind of binding effect, and can produce the sort of solidarity, that explain why self-interested citizens would place the demands of a "duty-imposing" state authority ahead of their own preferences. But is the phenomenon in need of explanation really being described correctly?

There is a remarkable dissonance between the rather archaic features of the "obligation potential" shared by comrades of fate who are willing to make sacrifices, on the one hand, and the normative self-understanding of the modern constitutional state as an uncoerced association of legal consociates, on the other. The examples of military duty, compulsory taxation, and education suggest a picture of the democratic state primarily as a duty-imposing authority demanding sacrifices from its dominated subjects. This picture fits poorly with an enlightenment culture whose normative core consists in the abolition of a publicly demanded *sacrificium* as an element of morality. The citizens of a democratic legal state understand themselves as the authors of the law, which compels them to obedience as its addressees. Unlike morality, positive law construes duties as something secondary; they arise only from the compatibility of the rights of each with the equal rights of all. Military duty (and capital punishment) cannot be defended on these premises. The duty to pay taxes follows from the decision to use coercive positive law as a medium for the construction of a political order whose first responsibility is to guarantee individual rights. And finally the so-called duty to education – mandatory primary and secondary education – is based on the fundamental right of children and young people to receive basic qualifications, a right that the state must carry out in the interests of the bearer of that basic right, if necessary even against the resistance of parents.

I am not overlooking the Janus-face of the "nation" as the first modern form of collective identity that nevertheless still drew its strength from projections of shared descent. The nation oscillates between the imaginary organicity of a *Volks-*

nation and the legal construct of a nation of citizens. But the
different paths that the emergence of nation-states has taken
in Europe – from state to nation in western and northern
Europe; from nation to state in central and eastern Europe –
attest to the constructed character of this new identity formation, mediated via law and mass communication. National consciousness owes its existence to the mobilization of
enfranchised voters in the political public sphere, no less than
to the mobilization of draftees in defense of the Fatherland. It
rests on the egalitarian self-understanding of democratic citizens, and arises from the communicative context of the press,
and from the discursive struggle for power of political parties.
In this heavily presuppositioned context, the nation-state
emerges as "the largest known social group that has ever managed to make the sacrifice of redistribution into a reasonable
demand."[78] But precisely the artificial conditions in which
national consciousness arose argue against the defeatist assumption that a form of civic solidarity among strangers can
only be generated within the confines of the nation.[79] If this
form of collective identity was due to a highly abstractive leap
from the local and dynastic to national and then to democratic
consciousness, why shouldn't this learning process be able to
continue?

This formal change of social integration will certainly not
come about automatically, through a functional integration
manufactured from economic interdependencies. Even if,
against all expectations, the European domestic market and
the common monetary policy can stabilize themselves without
political interventions to equalize growth and lower unemployment, such a systemic dynamic by itself would not be enough to
allow a form of mutual, transnational trust to emerge behind
the back, so to speak, of the cultural substrate. Another scen-
ario would be necessary for this, in which differing expectations
would mutually stimulate and support each other in a circular
process. A European Charter anticipates the transformed competencies that come with a constitution; but a constitution can
only function if the democratic process that it itself initiates
actually comes into being. This legitimation process has to be
supported by a European party system that can develop to the

degree that existing political parties, at first in their own respective national arenas, initiate a debate on the future of Europe,
and in the process articulate interests that cross national borders. And this debate, in turn, has to find a resonance in a pan-
European political public sphere that presupposes a European
civil society complete with interest groups, non-governmental
organizations, citizens' movements, and so forth. Transnational
mass media can only construct this multivocal communicative
context if, as is already the case in smaller countries, national
educational systems provide the basis of a common language –
even if in most cases it is a foreign language. The normative
impulses that first set these different processes in motion from
their scattered national sites will themselves only come about
through overlapping projects for a common political culture.[80]
But these projects can be constructed in the common historical
horizon that the citizens of Europe already find themselves in.

The learning process that can lead toward a European civil
solidarity encompasses a series of specifically European experiences. Since the end of the Middle Ages, developments in
Europe have been more strongly marked by divisions, differences, and tensions than in any other culture – by the rivalry
between secular and ecclesiastical powers, the regional fragmentation of political rule, the contradictions between town
and country, the schism of religious confessions and the deep
conflict between faith and knowledge, the competition of the
great powers, the imperial relation between "motherland" and
colonies, and above all by ambition and war between nations. In
happier moments, these sharp, often fatal, conflicts have acted
as a spur toward the decentering of perspectives; as an impulse
toward critical reflection on, and distancing from, prejudices
and biases; as a motive for the overcoming of particularisms,
toward tolerance and the institutionalization of disputes. These
experiences of successful forms of social integration have
shaped the normative self-understanding of European modernity into an egalitarian universalism that can ease the transition
to postnational democracy's demanding contexts of mutual
recognition for all of us – we, the sons, daughters, and grandchildren of a barbaric nationalism.

V

If based on nothing more than an expanded economic foundation and a unified currency, a European Federation could at best
aim for limited effects at isolated levels, for example creating
advantages for global competition. But the creation of larger
political unities in itself changes nothing about the mode of
locational competition as such; that is, the model of defensive
alliances against the rest of the world. On the other hand, such
supranational agreements at least meet a necessary condition
for politics to catch up with globalized markets. Thus at the
very least, a group of globally competent actors might emerge,
which in principle would be capable not just of broad agreements but also of their implementation. In closing I would like
to go into the question of whether such political actors, acting
within the framework of the United Nations, can strengthen an
initially very loose network of transnational agreements sufficiently to make a change of course toward a world domestic
policy possible without a world government.

At the global level, coordination problems that are already
difficult enough at the European level grow still sharper.
Because a negative coordination – refraining from taking measures – has the lowest possible implementation costs, the liberal-
ization of the world market (under the hegemonic pressure of
the United States) and the emergence of an international economic regime were ultimately successful in dismantling trade
barriers. The external effects of toxic waste production, and the
border-crossing risks of high technology, have even led to
organizations and practices that take over some regulatory
tasks. But the hurdles are still too high for the introduction of
global regulation, which would require not just a positive coordination of the actions of different governments, but an intervention in existing patterns of distribution as well.

In light of the most recent crises in Mexico and Asia, there is
naturally a growing interest in warding off stock market crashes,
and in strengthening regulations for credit transactions and
currency speculation. Critical events in the international finan-

cial markets point to the need for institutionalization. Moreover, globalized market commerce demands legal certainty, i.e. transnationally effective equivalents to the familiar guarantees of the private rights of citizens, which states grant to investors and trading partners within the national framework. "Deregulation can be seen as negotiating on the one hand the fact of globalization, and, on the other, the ongoing need for guarantees of contracts and property rights for which the state remains as the guarantor of last instance."[81] But just wishing for the regulatory powers of the state, whether for global financial markets or for the urban infrastructures and services that transnational businesses depend on, doesn't make the state either willing or able to undertake market-correcting regulations of this kind.[82] Under the conditions of global competition, national governments, incapable of macro-steering to influence the cycles of their increasingly de-nationalized "popular economies," have to limit themselves to improving the relative attractiveness of their local position, i.e. local conditions for capital valuation.

Influencing the mode of locational competition itself would be an entirely different matter. As things stand now, when it is not even possible to reach an agreement for a worldwide transaction tax on speculation profits, it is very hard to imagine any organization, standing conference, or indeed any procedure that the OECD states could agree to, for example, to serve as a framework for national taxation legislation. An international negotiating system that could place limits on the "race to the bottom" – the cost-cutting deregulatory race that reduces the capacities for social-political action and damages social standards – would need to enact and enforce redistributive regulations. Within a European Union that has assumed the character of a state, regardless of its multinational composition and the central roles of national governments, decisive policies of this sort would at least be conceivable. On the global level, however, both the competence for political action of a world government and a corresponding basis of legitimation are lacking. The United Nations is a loose community of states. It lacks the quality of a community of world citizens, who can legitimate their political decisions – and can make the consequences of those decisions into reasonable burdens for those affected – on the basis of a democratic opinion- and will-formation. Reflections on an order of world peace have occupied philosophers since the famous proposal of the Abbé Saint-Pierre (1729) until our own times, and they usually conclude with a warning about a despotic world rule.[83] But a look at the condition, the function, and the constitution of world organizations shows this worry to be groundless.

Today the United Nations unites member states that exhibit extreme differences in terms of population size and density, legitimation status, and level of economic development. In the UN General Assembly every member state has its own voice, while the composition of the Security Council and the voting rights of members take actual power relations into account. The United Nations' articles require national governments to observe human rights, to respect one another's sovereignty, and to refrain from the use of military force. With the criminalization of wars of aggression and crimes against humanity, nations, as the subjects of international law, have forfeited a general presumption of innocence. Of course, the United Nations has neither a standing international court of criminal justice (now in its planning stages in Rome) nor its own military forces at its disposal. But it can impose sanctions, and grant mandates for humanitarian interventions.

After the Second World War, the newly founded United Nations assumed the specific goal of preventing future wars. Its peacekeeping function was from the very beginning bound up with the task of the political enforcement of human rights. Since then, questions of environmental security have been added to this basic task of the prevention of war. But both the normative foundations of the UN Declaration on Human Rights, as well as the concentration on questions of security in the broadest sense, reveal the clearly limited functional responsibilities that the world organization, with no monopoly of violence, is charged with: controlling wars, civil wars and state-sponsored criminality on the one hand, and preventing humanitarian catastrophes and worldwide risks on the other. In view of this restriction to the basic services of maintaining order, even the most ambitious reforms of existing institutions would not lead in the direction of a world government.

The advocates of a "cosmopolitan democracy"[84] pursue three goals: first, the creation of a new political status of "world citizens," whose membership in world organizations would no longer be mediated through their nationality, but who would instead have popular representation in a world parliament through direct elections above the national level; second, the construction of a court of criminal justice with the usual competencies, whose decisions would be binding for national governments as well; finally, dismantling the UN Security Council in favor of a competent executive branch.[85] But even a world organization that has been expanded along these lines, and is operating on a broad basis of legitimacy, would be more or less effective only in restricted areas of competence, including reactive security and human rights policies, and preventive environmental policies.

The restriction to elementary services for maintaining order is a response not just to the pacifistic motivations that gave rise to the United Nations as a world organization in the first place. The world organization also lacks a basis of legitimacy on structural grounds. It is distinguished from state-organized communities by the principle of complete inclusion – it may exclude nobody, because it cannot permit any social boundaries between inside and outside. Any political community that wants to understand itself as a democracy must at least distinguish between members and non-members. The self-referential concept of collective self-determination demarcates a logical space for democratically united citizens who are members of a particular political community. Even if such a community is grounded in the universalist principles of a democratic constitutional state, it still forms a collective identity, in the sense that it interprets and realizes these principles in light of its own history and in the context of its own particular form of life. This ethical-political self-understanding of citizens of a particular democratic life is missing in the inclusive community of world citizens.[86]

Even if, despite this, world citizens were to organize themselves on a global level, and even if they created a form of democratically elected political representation, they would not be able to generate any normative cohesion from an ethical-political self-understanding that drew on other traditions and value orientations, but only from a legal-moral form of self-understanding. The normative model for a community that exists without any possible exclusions is the universe of moral persons – Kant's "kingdom of ends." It is thus no coincidence that "human rights," i.e. legal norms with an exclusively moral content,[87] make up the entire normative framework for a cosmopolitan community. This fact still doesn't predict whether the UN Declaration on Human Rights, whose wording was agreed on by the comparatively small number of founding members of the United Nations in 1946, could approach a unanimous interpretation and application in today's multicultural world. I cannot go into this cross-cultural discourse on human rights here.[88] But even a worldwide consensus on human rights could not serve as the basis for a strong equivalent to the *civic* solidarity that emerged in the framework of the nation-state. Civic solidarity is rooted in particular collective identities; cosmopolitan solidarity has to support itself on the moral universalism of human rights alone.

In comparison to the active solidarity among citizens, which among other things made the redistributive policies of the social welfare state tolerable, the solidarity of *world* citizens has a reactive character, insofar as it generates a kind of cosmopolitan cohesion in the first instance through feelings of indignation over the violations of rights, i.e. over repression and injuries to human rights committed by states. A legal community of world citizens that is all-inclusive yet organized in time and space certainly would be different from a universal community of moral persons, for which any such organization would be neither possible nor necessary. On the other hand, however, such a legal community of world citizens could not demand the comparatively firm levels of integration of state-organized communities with their own collective identities. I see no structural obstacles to expanding national civic solidarity and welfare-state policies to the scale of a postnational federation. But the political culture of a world society lacks the common ethical-political dimension that would be necessary for a corresponding global community – and its identity formation. At this point the objections that neo-Aristotelians have already raised against a national, let alone a European, constitutional patriotism come into play. A cosmopolitan community of world citizens can thus offer no adequate basis for a global domestic policy. The institutionalization of procedures for creating, generalizing, and coordinating global interests cannot take place within the organizational structure of a world state. Hence any plans for a "cosmopolitan democracy" will have to proceed according to another model.

A politics that can catch up with global markets, one that will be able to change the mode of locational competition, cannot simply be introduced at the top level of a multilevel politics organized into a "world state." Rather than a state, it has to find a less demanding basis of legitimacy in the organizational forms of an international negotiation system, which already exist today in other political arenas. In general, procedures and accords require a sort of compromise between independent actors who have the ability to impose sanctions to compel consideration of their respective interests. In a politically constituted community organized via a state, this compromise formation is more closely meshed with procedures of deliberative politics, so that agreements are not simply produced by an equalization of interests in terms of power politics. Within the framework of a common political culture, negotiation partners also have recourse to common value orientations and shared conceptions of justice, which make an understanding beyond instrumental-rational agreements possible. But on the international level this "thick" communicative embeddedness is missing. And a "naked" compromise formation that simply reflects back the essential features of classical power politics is an inadequate beginning for a world domestic policy. Naturally, procedures for intergovernmental accords are not dependent on given constellations of power alone. As normative framing conditions delimit the choice of rhetorical strategies, they effectively structure negotiations just as much as the influence of "epistemic communities" (which occasionally generate thoroughly normative, global background consensuses over supposedly purely scientific questions, as in the case of today's neoliberal economic regime). Global powers no longer operate in the state of nature envisioned by classical international law, but on the middle level of an emerging world politics.

This presents a diffuse picture – not the stable picture of a multilevel politics *within* a world organization, but rather the dynamic picture of interferences and interactions *between* political processes that persist at national, international, and global levels. The international negotiating systems that make agreements between state actors possible communicate on the one side with internal state processes that respective governments depend on; on the other side they also connect up with the contexts and policies of the world organization. The result is at least a prospect for a world domestic policy without a world government – provided that two problems can be clarified. The first problem is more fundamental; the second is empirical. (a) How can we envision the democratic legitimation of decisions beyond the schema of the nation-state? And (b), what are the conditions for a transformed self-understanding of global actors in which states and supranational regimes begin to see themselves as members of a community, who have no choice but to consider one another's interests mutually, and to perceive general interests?

(a) Both the liberal and the republican traditions understand the political participation of citizens in an essentially voluntaristic sense: all should have the same chance to voice their own preferences or their political will in an effective way, be it in pursuit of their private interests (Locke), or in the exercise of their political autonomy (Mill). But if we also ascribe an epistemic function to democratic will-formation, the pursuit of self-interest and the realization of political freedom are supplemented by a further dimension, the public use of reason (Kant). Accordingly, the democratic procedure no longer draws its legitimizing force only, indeed not even predominantly, from political participation and the expression of political will, but rather from the general accessibility of a deliberative process whose structure grounds an expectation of rationally acceptable results.[89] Such a discourse-theoretical understanding of democracy changes the theoretical demands placed on the legitimacy conditions for democratic politics. A functioning public sphere, the quality of discussion, accessibility, and the discursive structure of opinion- and will-formation: all of these could never entirely replace conventional procedures for decision-making and political representation. But they do tip the balance, from the concrete embodiments of sovereign will in persons, votes, and collectives to the procedural demands of communicative and decision-making processes. And this loosens the conceptual ties between democratic legitimacy and the familiar forms of state organization.

Supposedly weak forms of legitimation then appear in another light.[90] For example, the institutionalized participation of non-governmental organizations in the deliberations of international negotiating systems would strengthen the legitimacy of the procedure insofar as mid-level transnational decision-making processes could then be rendered transparent for national public spheres, and thus be reconnected with decision-making procedures at the grassroots level. And equipping the world organization with the right to demand that member states carry out referendums on important issues at any time is also an interesting suggestion under discourse-theoretical premises.[91] As in the cases of UN summit conferences on environmental threats, equal rights for women, disputed interpretations of human rights, global poverty, etc., this might at least force a discussion on how best to regulate issues that would otherwise remain invisible and would never make it onto the political agenda.

(b) Of course, a renewed political closure of an economically unmastered world society would be possible only if global powers also involve themselves in the institutionalized procedures for building a transnational will-formation regarding the preservation of social standards and the redress of extreme social inequities. They have to be willing to broaden their perspectives on what counts as the "national interest" into a viewpoint of "global governance." But this changed perspective, from "international relations" to a world domestic policy, cannot be expected from governments if their populations themselves do not reward them for it. The governing elites have to concern themselves with consensus and re-election within their own national arenas; thus they ought not to be punished for operating on the cooperative procedures of a cosmopolitan community rather than those of national independence. Innovations will not happen if the political elites cannot find any resonance with the already transformed value orientations of their electorates. But if the self-understanding of governments only changes under the pressure of an altered domestic climate, then the crucial question is whether, in the civil societies and political public spheres of increasingly interconnected regimes, whether here, in Europe and in the Federal Republic of Germany, a cosmopolitan consciousness – the consciousness of a compulsory cosmopolitan solidarity, so to speak – will arise.

The re-regulation of the world society has, until now, not even taken the shape of an exemplary project for which one could provide examples. Its first addressees are not governments but citizens, and citizens' movements. But social movements crystallize around normatively liberating perspectives for resolving conflicts that had previously appeared insoluble. The articulation of a vision is also the task of political parties that have not yet entirely withdrawn from civil society and barricaded themselves into the political system. Parties that don't simply cling to the status quo need a perspective that moves beyond it. And the status quo today is nothing other than the whirlpool of an accelerating process of modernization that has been left to its own devices. The political parties that are still able to exert any formative influence also have to muster the courage for forward thinking in other respects. Within the national sphere – the only one that they can currently operate in – they have to reach out toward a European arena of action. And this arena, in turn, has to be programmatically opened up with the dual objective of creating a social Europe that can throw its weight onto the cosmopolitan scale.

5

Remarks on Legitimation through Human Rights

In this essay I use the term "legitimation" (and the associated term "legitimacy") in a doubly restricted sense: I am referring, first, to the legitimation of political systems and, second, only to the legitimation of constitutional democracies. I begin by recalling a proposal I have made for reconstructing the internal relation between democracy and human rights.[1] I then briefly examine a few of the aspects under which this Western style of legitimation is criticized today – whether in the discourse among Western theorists or in the discourses between other cultures and the West.

I. The Procedural Justification of Constitutional Democracy

Let me begin by explicating the concept of political legitimation. Social orders in which authority is organized through a state – orders that can, for example, be distinguished from tribal societies – experience a need for legitimation that is already implicit in the concept of political power. Because the medium of state power is constituted in forms of law, political orders draw their recognition from the legitimacy claim of law. That is, law requires more than mere acceptance; besides demanding that its addressees give it *de facto* recognition, the law claims to *deserve* their recognition. Consequently, all the public justifications and constructions that are intended to redeem this claim to worthiness of recognition are part of the legitimation of a government constituted through law.

This holds for all governments. Modern states are characterized by the fact that political power is constituted in the form of positive law, which is to say: enacted and coercive law. Because the question regarding the mode of political legitimation is bound up with this legal form, I would like first to delineate modern law by describing its structure and mode of validity. Only then can I discuss the kind of legitimation associated with such law.

(1) Individual rights make up the core of modern legal orders. By opening up the legal space for pursuing personal preferences, individual rights release the entitled person from moral precepts and other prescriptions in a carefully circumscribed manner. In any case, within the boundaries of what is legally permitted no one is legally obligated to publicly justify her action. With the introduction of individual liberties, modern law – in contrast to traditional legal orders – validates the Hobbesian principle that whatever is not explicitly prohibited is permitted.[2] Whereas morality primarily tells us what our obligations are, law has a structure that gives primacy to entitlements. Whereas moral rights are derived from reciprocal duties, legal duties stem from the legal constraints on individual liberties. This conceptual privileging of rights over duties is implicit in the modern concepts of the legal person and the legal community. The moral universe, which is unlimited in social space and historical time, includes all natural persons with all the complexities of their life histories. By contrast, a legal community, which has a spatio-temporal location, protects the integrity of its members only insofar as they acquire the artificial status of bearers of individual rights.

This structure is reflected by the law's peculiar mode of validity. In the legal mode of validity we find the facticity of the state's enforcement and implementation of law intertwined with the legitimacy of the purportedly rational procedure of lawmaking. Modern law leaves its addressees free to approach the law in either of two ways. They can consider norms merely as factual constraints on their freedom and take a strategic

approach to the calculable consequences of possible rule-viola-
tions, or they can comply with the regulation "out of respect
for the law." Kant already expressed this point with his concept
of legality, which highlighted the connection between these
two moments without which legal obedience cannot be reasonably expected of morally responsible persons. Legal norms must
be so fashioned that they can be viewed simultaneously in two
different ways, as laws of coercion and as laws of freedom. It
must at least be possible to obey laws not because they are
compulsory but because they are legitimate. The validity of a
legal norm means that the state guarantees both legitimate
lawmaking and *de facto* enforcement. The state must ensure
both of these: on the one hand, the legality of behavior in the
sense of an average compliance that is, if necessary, enforced
through penalties; on the other hand, a legitimacy of legal rules
that always makes it possible to comply with a norm out of
respect for the law.

However, for the legitimacy of the legal order another formal
characteristic is especially important, namely the positivity of
enacted law. How can we ground the legitimacy of rules that are
always able to be changed by the political legislator? Constitutional norms too are changeable; even the basic norms that the
Constitution itself has declared non-amendable share, along with
all positive law, the fate that they can be abrogated, say, after a
change of regime. As long as one was able to fall back on a
religiously or metaphysically grounded natural law, the whirlpool of temporality enveloping positive law could be held in
check by morality. Even temporalized positive law was at first
supposed to remain subordinate to, and be permanently oriented
by, the eternally valid moral law, which was conceived of as a
"higher law." But in pluralistic societies such integrating worldviews and collectively binding ethical systems have disintegrated.

Political theory has given a twofold answer to the question of
legitimacy: popular sovereignty and human rights. The principle of popular sovereignty lays down a procedure that,
because of its democratic features, justifies the presumption
of legitimate outcomes. This principle is expressed in the rights
of communication and participation that secure the public
autonomy of politically enfranchised citizens. The classical

human rights, by contrast, ground an inherently legitimate rule of law. These rights guarantee the life and private liberty – that is, scope for the pursuit of personal life-plans – of citizens. Popular sovereignty and human rights provide the two normative perspectives from which an enacted, changeable law is supposed to be legitimated as a means to secure both the private and civic autonomy of the individual.

(2) However, political philosophy has never really been able to strike a balance between popular sovereignty and human rights, or between the "freedom of the ancients" and the "freedom of the moderns." Republicanism, which goes back to Aristotle and the political humanism of the Renaissance, has always given the public autonomy of citizens priority over the pre-political liberties of private persons. Liberalism, which goes back to John Locke, has invoked (at least since the nineteenth century) the danger of tyrannical majorities and postulated the priority of human rights. According to republicanism, human rights owed their legitimacy to the ethical self-understanding and sovereign self-determination achieved by a political community; in liberalism, such rights were supposed to provide inherently legitimate barriers that prevented the sovereign will of the people from encroaching on inviolable spheres of individual freedom. In opposition to the complementary one-sidedness of these two traditions, one must insist that the idea of human rights – Kant's fundamental right to equal individual liberties – must neither be merely imposed on the sovereign legislator as an external barrier nor be instrumentalized as a functional requisite for democratic self-determination.[3]

To express this intuition properly, in what follows I start with the following question: What basic rights must free and equal citizens mutually accord one another if they want to regulate their common life legitimately by means of positive law? This idea of a constitution-making practice links the expression of popular sovereignty with the creation of a system of rights. Here I assume a principle that I cannot discuss in detail, namely, that a law may claim legitimacy only if all those possibly affected could consent to it after participating in rational discourses. As participants in "discourses," we want to arrive at shared opinions by mutually convincing one another about some issue through arguments, whereas in "bargaining" we strive for a balance of different interests. (One should note, however, that the fairness of bargained agreements depends in turn on discursively justified procedures of compromise formation.) Now, if discourses (and bargaining processes) are the place where a reasonable political will can develop, then the presumption of legitimate outcomes, which the democratic procedure is supposed to justify, ultimately rests on an elaborate communicative arrangement: the forms of communication necessary for a reasonable will-formation of the political lawgiver, the conditions that ensure legitimacy, must be legally institutionalized.

The desired internal relation between human rights and popular sovereignty consists in this: human rights institutionalize the communicative conditions for a reasonable political will-formation. Rights, which make the exercise of popular sovereignty possible, cannot be imposed on this practice like external constraints. To be sure, this claim is immediately plausible only for political rights, that is, the rights of communication and participation; it is not so obvious for the classical human rights that guarantee the citizen's private autonomy. The human rights that guarantee everyone a comprehensive legal protection and an equal opportunity to pursue her private life-plans clearly have an intrinsic value. They are not reducible to their instrumental value for democratic will-formation.

At the same time, we must not forget that the medium through which citizens exercise their political autonomy is not a matter of choice. Citizens participate in legislation only as *legal* subjects; it is no longer in their power to decide which language they will make use of. Hence the legal code as such must already be available before the communicative presuppositions of a discursive will-formation can be institutionalized in the form of civil rights. To establish this legal code, however, it is necessary to create the status of legal persons who as bearers of individual rights belong to a voluntary association of citizens and can, when necessary, effectively claim their rights. There is no law without the private autonomy of legal persons in general. Consequently, without the classical liberty rights, in particular the basic right to equal individual liberties, there also would not be any medium in which to legally institutionalize the conditions under which citizens could participate in the practice of self-determination.

This shows how private and public autonomy reciprocally presuppose one another. The internal relation between democracy and the rule of law consists in this: on the one hand, citizens can make appropriate use of their public autonomy only if, on the basis of their equally protected private autonomy, they are sufficiently independent; on the other hand, they can realize equality in the enjoyment of their private autonomy only if they make appropriate use of their political autonomy as citizens. Consequently, liberal and political basic rights are inseparable. The image of kernel and husk is misleading – as though there were a core area of elementary liberty rights that would have priority over rights of communication and participation.[4] For the Western style of legitimation, the co-originality of liberty rights and the rights of citizens is essential.

II.   The Self-criticism of the West

Human rights are Janus-faced, looking simultaneously toward morality and the law. Their moral content notwithstanding, they have the form of legal rights. Like moral norms, they refer to every creature "that bears a human face," but as legal norms they protect individual persons only insofar as the latter belong to a particular legal community – normally the citizens of a nation-state. Thus a peculiar tension arises between the universal meaning of human rights and the local conditions of their realization: they should have unlimited validity for all persons – but how is that to be achieved? On the one hand, one can imagine the global expansion of human rights in such a way that all existing states are transformed – and not just in name only – into constitutional democracies, while each individual receives the right to a nationality of his or her choice. We are obviously a long way from achieving this goal. An alternative route would emerge if each individual attained the effective enjoyment of human rights immediately, as a world citizen. In this sense, Article 28 of the United Nations Declaration of Human Rights refers to a global order "in which the rights and freedoms set forth in this Declaration can be fully realized," but even the goal of an actually institutionalized cosmopolitan legal order lies in the distant future.

In the transition from nation-states to a cosmopolitan order, it is hard to say which poses the greater danger: the disappearing world of sovereign subjects of international law, who lost their innocence long ago, or the ambiguous mish-mash of supranational institutions and conferences, which can grant a dubious legitimation but which depend as always on the good will of powerful states and alliances.[5] In this volatile situation, human rights provide the sole recognized basis of legitimation for the politics of the international community; nearly every state has by now accepted, at least on paper, the United Nations Declaration of Human Rights. Nevertheless, the general validity, content, and ranking of human rights are as contested as ever. Indeed, the human rights discourse that has been argued on normative terms is plagued by the fundamental doubt about whether the form of legitimation that has arisen in the West can also hold up as plausible within the frameworks of other cultures. The most radical critics are Western intellectuals themselves. They maintain that the universal validity claimed for human rights merely hides a perfidious claim to power on the part of the West.

This is no accident. To gain some distance from one's own traditions and to broaden limited perspectives is one of the advantages of occidental rationalism. The European history of the interpretation and realization of human rights is the history of such a decentering of our way of viewing things. So-called equal rights may have only been gradually extended to oppressed, marginalized, and excluded groups. Only after tough political struggles have workers, women, Jews, Romanies, gays, and political refugees been recognized as "human beings" with a claim to fully equal treatment. The important thing now is that the individual advances in emancipation reveal in hindsight the ideological function that human rights had also fulfilled up to that time. That is, the egalitarian claim to universal validity and inclusion had also always served to mask the *de facto* unequal treatment of those who were silently excluded. This observation has aroused the suspicion that human rights might be reducible to this ideological function. Have they not always served to shield a false universality – an imaginary humanity, behind which an imperialistic West could conceal its own way and interests? Following Martin Heidegger and Carl Schmitt, Western intellectuals have read this hermeneutic of suspicion in two ways, as a critique of reason and as a critique of power.

According to the first reading, the idea of human rights is the expression of a specifically Western notion of reason that has its origins in Platonism. Spurred by an "abstractive fallacy," this notion leaps beyond the boundaries of its original context of emergence, thus exceeding the merely local validity of its alleged universality. The critique of reason contends that every tradition, worldview, or culture has inscribed its own – always incommensurable – standards for what is true and false. But this leveling critique fails to notice the peculiar self-referential character of the discourse of modernity. The discourse of human rights is also set up to provide *every* voice with a hearing. Consequently, this discourse itself sets the standards in whose light the latent violations of its own claims can be discovered and corrected. Lutz Wingert has called this the "detective aspect" of human rights discourses: human rights, which demand the inclusion of the other, function at the same time as sensors for exclusionary practices exercised in their name.[6]

The variants of the critique of power proceed somewhat more awkwardly. They too deny the claim to universal validity by referring to the genetic priority of a suppressed particularity. But this time a reductionistic feint suffices. The normative language of law can supposedly reflect nothing else but the factual claims to power of political self-assertion; according to this view, consequently, universal legal claims always conceal the particular will of a specific collectivity to have its own way. But the critics of power forget that the more fortunate nations learned in the eighteenth century how sheer power can be domesticated by legitimate law. "He who says 'humanity' is lying" – this familiar piece of German ideology only betrays a lack of historical experience.[7]

Western intellectuals should not confuse their discourse over their own Eurocentric biases with the debates in which members of other cultures engage them. True, in the cross-cultural discourse we also encounter arguments that the spokespersons of other cultures have borrowed from European critics in order to show that the validity of human rights remains imprisoned, despite everything, in the original European context. But those non-Western critics, whose self-consciousness comes from their own traditions, certainly do not reject human rights lock, stock, and barrel. The reason is that other cultures and world religions are now also exposed to the challenges of social modernity, just as Europe was in its day, when it in some sense "discovered" or "invented" human rights and constitutional democracy.

In what follows I will take the apologetic role of a Western participant in a cross-cultural discussion of human rights. My working hypothesis is that the standards of human rights stem less from the particular cultural background of Western civilization than from the attempt to answer specific challenges posed by a social modernity that has in the meantime covered the globe. However we evaluate this modern starting point, human rights confront us today with fact that leaves us no choice and thus neither requires, nor is capable of, a retrospective justification. The contest over the adequate interpretation of human rights concerns not the desirability of the "modern condition," but rather an interpretation of human rights that does justice to the modern world from the viewpoint of other cultures as well as our own. The controversy turns above all on the individualism and secular character of human rights that are centered in the concept of autonomy.

For the purposes of clarity I base my metacritical remarks on a description that provides a frank expression of the Western standards of legitimacy. The above reconstruction of the relation between liberty rights and the rights of citizens starts from a situation in which we assume that free and equal citizens take counsel together on how they can regulate their common life not only by means of positive law but also legitimately. I recall in advance three implications of this proposal, which are relevant for the further course of the argument:

(a) This model begins with the horizontal relationships that citizens have with one another. Only in a second step, and thus only on an established rights basis, does the model introduce the relationships that citizens have to the functionally necessary state apparatus. This allows us to avoid the liberal fixation on the question of how one controls the state's monopoly on force. Although the liberal question is understandable from the perspective of European history, it shoves the more innocuous question about the solidaristic justification of a political community into the background.

(b) In the model I propose, the starting question assumes that we can take the medium of enacted, coercible law more or less at face value as effective and unproblematic. Unlike classical contract theory, the proposed model does not treat the creation of an association of legal persons, defined as bearers of individual rights, as a decision in need of normative justification. A functional account suffices as justification, because complex societies, whether Asian or European, seem to have no functional equivalent for the integrative achievements of law. This kind of artificially created norm, at once compulsory and freedom-guaranteeing, has also proven its worth for producing an abstract form of civic solidarity among strangers who want to remain strangers.

(c) Finally, the model of constitution-making is understood in such a way that human rights are not pregiven moral truths to be discovered but rather are constructions. Unlike moral rights, legal rights, quite clearly, must not remain politically non-binding. As individual or "subjective" rights, human rights have an inherently juridical nature and are conceptually oriented toward positive enactment by legislative bodies.

These reflections change nothing about the individualistic style and secular basis of legal systems based on human rights; indeed, they emphasize the centrality accorded to autonomy. At the same time, however, they cast a different light on the criticisms one hears in the cross-cultural discourse, which targets both aspects of Western legal systems.

III. The Discourse between the West and other Cultures: "Asiatic Values"

As became evident at the Vienna Conference on Human Rights, a debate has got underway since the 1991 report of the Singapore government on "Shared Values" and the 1993 Bangkok Declaration jointly signed by Singapore, Malaysia, Taiwan, and China. In this debate the strategic statements of government representatives are in part allied with, and in part clash with, the contributions of oppositional and independent intellectuals. The objections are essentially directed against the individualistic character of human rights. The critique, which invokes the indigenous "values" of far-eastern cultures shaped by Confucianism, moves along three lines. Specifically, the critics (1) question the principled priority of rights over duties, (2) appeal to a particular communitarian "hierarchy" of human rights, and (3) lament the negative effects that an individualistic legal order has on the social cohesion of the community.

(1) The core of the debate lies in the thesis that the ancient cultures of Asia (as well as the tribal cultures of Africa[8]) accord priority to the community over the individual and do not recognize a sharp separation between law and ethics. The political community is traditionally integrated more by duties than by rights. The political ethic recognizes no individual rights, but only rights that are conferred on individuals. For this reason, the individualistic legal understanding of the West is supposedly incompatible with the community-based ethos that is deeply anchored in a particular tradition and that requires individual conformity and subordination.[9]

It seems to me that the debate takes a false turn with this reference to cultural differences. In fact, one can infer the function of modern law from its form. Individual rights provide a kind of protective belt for the individual's private conduct of life, and in two ways: rights protect the conscientious pursuit of an ethical life-project just as much as they secure an orientation toward personal preferences free of moral scrutiny. This legal form is tailored to the functional demands of modern economic societies, which rely on the decentralized decisions of numerous independent actors. However, Asiatic societies too deploy positive law as a steering medium in the framework of a globalized system of market relations. They do so for the same functional reasons that once allowed this form of law to prevail in the Occident over the older guild-based forms of social integration. Legal certainty, for example, is one of the necessary conditions for a commerce based on predictability, accountability, and the preservation of trust. Consequently, the decisive alternatives lie not at the cultural but at the socioeconomic level. Asiatic societies cannot participate in capitalistic modernization without taking advantage of the achievements of an individualistic legal order. One cannot desire the one and reject the other. From the perspective of Asian countries, the question is not whether human rights, as part of an individualistic legal order, are compatible with the transmission of one's own culture. Rather, the question is whether the traditional forms of political and societal integration can be reasserted against – or must instead be adapted to – the hard-to-resist imperatives of an economic modernization that has won approval on the whole.

(2) These reservations about European individualism are often expressed not for normative reasons but with a strategic intention. This intention can be recognized insofar as the arguments are connected with the political justification of the more or less "soft" authoritarianism that characterizes the dictatorships of developing nations. This is especially true of the dispute over the hierarchy of human rights. The governments of Singapore, Malaysia, Taiwan, and China appeal to a "priority" of social and cultural basic rights in an effort to justify the violations against basic legal and political rights of which the West accuses them. These dictatorships consider themselves authorized by the "right of social development" – apparently understood as a collective right – to postpone the realization of liberal rights and rights of political participation until their countries have attained a level of economic development that allows them to satisfy the basic material needs of the population equally. For a population in misery, they claim, legal equality and freedom of

opinion are not so relevant as the prospect of better living conditions.

One cannot convert functional arguments into normative ones this easily. True, some conditions are more beneficial than others for the long-term implementation of human rights. But that does not justify an authoritarian model of development, according to which the freedom of the individual is subordinated to the "good of the community" as it is paternalistically apprehended and defined. In reality, these governments do not defend individual rights at all, but rather a paternalistic care meant to allow them to restrict rights that in the West have been considered the most basic (the rights to life and bodily integrity, the rights to comprehensive legal protection and equal treatment, to religious freedom, freedom of association, free speech, and so forth). From a normative standpoint, according "priority" to social and cultural basic rights does not make sense for the simple reason that such rights only serve to secure the "fair value" (Rawls) of liberal and political basic rights, i.e. the factual presuppositions for the equal opportunity to exercise individual rights.[10]

(3) The two arguments above are often linked with a critique of the suspected effects of an individualistic legal order, which appears to endanger the integrity of the naturally emergent living systems of family, neighborhoods, and politics. According to this critique, a legal order that equips persons with actionable individual rights is set up for conflict and thus at odds with the orientation of the indigenous culture toward consensus. It helps if we distinguish the principled reading of this criticism from a political reading.

From the principled point of view, the reservations about the individualistic style of European human rights are backed by the justified critique of an understanding of rights that stems from the Lockean tradition and that has been revived today by neoliberalism. This possessive individualism fails to recognize that legally protected individual rights can only be derived from the pre existing, indeed intersubjectively recognized norms of a legal community. It is true that individual rights are parts of the equipment of legal persons; but the status of legal persons as rights-bearers develops only in the context of a legal community which is premised on the mutual recognition of its freely associated members. Consequently, the understanding of human rights must jettison the metaphysical assumption of an individual who exists prior to all socialization and, as it were, comes into the world already equipped with innate rights. However, dropping this "Western" thesis also makes its "Eastern" antithesis unnecessary – that the claims of the legal community have priority over individual legal claims. The choice between "individualist" and "collectivist" approaches disappears once we approach fundamental legal concepts with an eye toward the dialectical unity of individuation and socialization processes. Because even legal persons are individuated only on the path to socialization, the integrity of individual persons can be protected only together with the free access to those interpersonal relationships and cultural traditions in which they can maintain their identities. Without this kind of "communitarianism," a properly understood individualism remains incomplete.

In contrast to the principled critique, the political objection to the disintegrating effects of modern law is rather weak. The processes of economic and social modernization, which are both accelerated and violent in the developing nations, must not be confused with the legal forms in which social disintegration, exploitation, and the abuse of administrative power occur. The only means of countering the factual oppression exercised by the dictatorships of developing nations is a juridification of politics. The integration problems that every highly complex society has to master can be solved by means of modern law, however, only if legitimate law helps to generate that abstract form of civic solidarity that stands and falls with the realization of basic rights.[11]

IV.   The Challenge of Fundamentalism

The attack on the individualism of human rights targets one aspect of the underlying concept of autonomy, namely the liberties that are guaranteed to private citizens *vis-à-vis* the state and third parties. But citizens are autonomous in a political sense only when they give themselves their laws. The model of a constitutional assembly points toward a constructivist conception of basic rights. Kant conceived autonomy as the capacity to bind one's own will by normative insights that result from the public use of reason. This idea of self-legislation also inspires the procedure of democratic will-formation that makes it possible to base political authority on a mode of legitimation that is neutral toward worldviews. As a result, a religious or metaphysical justification of human rights becomes superfluous. To this extent, the secularization of politics is simply the flip-side of the political autonomy of citizens.

The European conception of human rights is open to attack by the spokespersons of other cultures not only because the concept of autonomy gives human rights an individualistic character, but also because autonomy implies a secularized political authority uncoupled from religious or cosmological worldviews. In the view of Islamic, Christian, or Jewish fundamentalists, their own truth claim is absolute in the sense that it deserves to be enforced even by means of political power, if necessary. This outlook has consequences for the exclusive character of the polity; legitimations based on religions or worldviews of this sort are incompatible with the inclusion of equally entitled non-believers or persons of other persuasions.

However, a profane legitimation through human rights, and thus the uncoupling of politics from divine authority, poses a provocative challenge not only for fundamentalists. Indian intellectuals, such as Ashis Nandy, have also written "anti-secularization manifestoes."[12] They expect the mutual toleration and cross-fertilization of Islamic and Hindu religious cultures to develop more from a reciprocal interpenetration of the modes of religious perception of both cultures than from the neutrality of the state toward worldviews. They are skeptical about an official politics of neutrality that merely neutralizes the public meaning of religion. Such considerations, however, combine the normative question — how one can find a shared basis for a just political life in common – with an empirical question. The differentiation of a religious sphere separate from the state may in fact weaken the influence of privatized "gods and demons." But the principle of toleration itself is not directed against the authenticity and truth claims of religious confessions and forms of life; rather, its sole purpose is to enable their equally entitled coexistence within the same political community.

The central issue in the controversy cannot be described as a dispute over the relevance that different cultures each give to religion. The conception of human rights was the answer to a problem that once confronted Europeans – when they had to overcome the political consequences of confessional fragmentation – and now confronts other cultures in a similar fashion. In any event, the conflict of cultures takes place today in the framework of a world society in which the collective actors must, regardless of their different cultural traditions, agree for better or worse on norms of coexistence. The autarkic isolation against external influences is no longer an option in today's world. However, the pluralism of worldviews is also breaking out inside societies that are still conditioned by strong traditions.

Even in societies that, culturally speaking, are comparatively homogenous, a reflexive reformulation of the prevailing dogmatic traditions is increasingly hard to avoid.[13] The awareness is growing, first of all among the intellectuals, that one's own religious truths must be brought into conformity with publicly recognized secular knowledge and defended before other religious truth claims in the same universe of discourse. Like Christianity since the Reformation, traditional worldviews are thus being transformed into "reasonable comprehensive doctrines" under the reflexive pressure generated by modern life circumstances. This is how Rawls designates an ethical worldview and self-understanding that has become reflexive, open to reasonable disagreement with other belief systems, but also able to reach an understanding with them on the rules of equal coexistence.[14]

My apologetic reflections present the Western mode of legitimation as an answer to general challenges that are no longer simply problems just for Western civilization. Naturally, this does not mean that the answer found by the West is the only one or even the best one. To this extent, the current debate provides us with an opportunity to become aware of our own blind spots. However, hermeneutical reflection on the starting point of a human rights discourse among participants of different cultures draws our attention to normative contents that are present in the tacit presuppositions of any discourse whose goal is mutual understanding. That is, independently of their cultural backgrounds all the participants intuitively know quite well that a consensus based on conviction cannot come about as long as symmetrical relations do not exist among them – relations of mutual recognition, mutual role-taking, a shared willingness to consider one's own tradition with the eyes of the stranger and to learn from one another, and so forth. On this basis, we can criticize not only selective readings, tendentious interpretations, and narrow-minded applications of human rights, but also that shameless instrumentalization of human rights that conceals particular interests behind a universalistic mask – a deception that leads one to the false assumption that the meaning of human rights is exhausted by their misuse.

6

Conceptions of Modernity
A Look Back at Two Traditions

When a philosophical society invites me to give an address on "conceptions of modernity," they do so on the (by no means trivial) presupposition that "modernity" is a legitimate topic for philosophy.[1] This reminds us of the classical conception of the modern, first articulated by Hegel, and developed in the social theories of Marx, Max Weber, the young Lukács, and the early Frankfurt School. In the end, this tradition suffocated in the aporetic self-referentiality of a totalizing critique of reason; since then, the project of a self-critical self-reassurance of modernity has been carried on with the help of a different concept of a linguistically embodied, "situated" reason. Of course, two competing versions have emerged from this linguistic turn: the postmodern "overcoming" of the normative self-understanding of modernity on the one hand, and the intersubjectivistic reformulation of the classical conception of an ambiguous modernity on the other.

I

I would like to begin by explaining why it was that "the modern" became a topic for philosophy in the first place. Precisely speaking, this is a matter of three separate questions: (1) When, and why, did philosophers become interested in an interpretation of the specific condition of modernity? (2) Why do these philosophical interpretations take the form of a critique of reason? (3) Why did philosophy ultimately cede the ongoing task of an interpretation of modernity to social theory?

(1) The word "modernus" was first used in the late fifth century to distinguish what had become a "Christian" present from a "pagan" Roman past.[2] Ever since, the term has carried the connotation of a deliberate break between the new and the old. Time and again, the term "modern" was employed – always within a different context – to articulate the consciousness of a new epoch. Initially, this distancing from the immediate past functioned by hearkening back to antiquity, or to any other period designated as "classical" and hence worthy of imitation. The Renaissance, with which our own conception of the "modern age" begins, referred back to classical Greece in this manner. Around 1800, however, a group of young writers opposed this usage by setting the classical in opposition to the romantic, envisioning an idealized medieval period as their own normative past. This romantic consciousness also showed the distinctive features of a new beginning, detaching itself from what it supposed it was leaving behind. Because the tradition that is to be surpassed still continues into the present, the "modern" spirit has to devalue its own immediate prehistory, distancing itself from it as a way of grounding itself normatively from its own resources.

The celebrated *querrelle des anciens et des moderns* – the dispute with the protagonists of a classical aesthetics in France of the late seventeenth century – indicates how art and aesthetic experience prepared the ground for an understanding of "modernity." Each period produced its own style, long before the self-understanding of the twentieth century avant-garde accelerated and institutionalized stylistic change. In the artistic sphere, the intensified awareness of self-produced discontinuities is hardly surprising. But with the close of the eighteenth century a new, general historical consciousness arose that, in the end, seized even philosophy itself. Hegel is explicit in identifying the "break" that the French Revolution and the Enlightenment signified for the more thoughtful of his contemporaries.[3]

For this new consciousness, the "modern" now stands opposed to the "old" world insofar as it is radically open to the future. The transient moment of the present thus gains significance as the point of departure for each new generation's embrace of the whole of history. Even the term "history" in the singular is, in contrast to the many histories of different actors, a coinage of the late eighteenth century.[4] History is now experienced as an all-encompassing, problem-generating process, and time as a scarce resource for mastering the problems that the future hurls at the present. This headlong rush of challenges is perceived as the "pressure of time."

This modern time consciousness has a peculiar effect on philosophy. Earlier, philosophy – indeed theory as such – was supposed to provide a true representation of the essence of the world; of the universal, necessary, and eternal features of reality as such. But as soon as philosophy is obliged to reflect on its own historical position, theory – the grasp of truth – receives a temporal index. In the worldly horizon of the present, the source of fleeting, contingent, and ever more particular events, the context of justification becomes interwoven with the context of discovery. If true philosophical insights are nevertheless to claim a context-transcendent validity, then philosophy must grasp and penetrate this disquieting present, and articulate it in concepts. Philosophy can only seek to overcome the boundaries of the historical situation which philosophical thought itself occupies by conceiving "the modern" as such. Hegel was the first philosopher to articulate this new requirement of "grasping one's own time in thought." Philosophy must meet the challenge of time with an analysis of the "new age." But why should it, how could it, conceive modernity through the means of a critique of reason?

(2) Because modernity understands itself in opposition to tradition, it seeks a foothold for itself, so to speak, in reason. Even if those who regarded themselves as modern had always invented an idealized past as an object for imitation, as modernity grew self-reflective it was obliged to justify its choice of models according to its own standards, and create all its normativity from out of itself. Modernity had to stabilize itself through

its own authority, the only authority remaining: that of reason. For only in the name of Enlightenment was it able to devalue and overcome tradition. On the basis of this affinity, Hegel understood modernity's need for self-reassurance as the "need for philosophy." As the custodian of reason, philosophy conceives modernity as a child of the Enlightenment.

Since Descartes, modern philosophy focussed on subjectivity and self-consciousness. It explained reason through the concept of the self-referentiality of a knowing subject, which bent back upon itself, so to speak, in order to catch sight of its own mirror image *as* a knowing subject. Mind possesses itself through an act of self-reflection that reveals consciousness as a sphere, not of objects but of the representation of objects. Hegel adopts this "speculative model of reason" in order to characterize the modern age through a principle of subjectivity, a principle that grants freedom through reflection: "The greatness of our age rests in the fact that freedom, the peculiar possession of mind whereby it is at home with itself in itself, is recognized."[5] Subjectivity is a foundational, indeed in a certain sense a fundamentalist, concept. It provides a mode of evidence, and certainty, on whose basis everything else can be doubted and criticized. Thus modernity prides itself on its critical spirit, which accepts nothing as self-evident except in light of good reasons. "Subjectivity" has both a universalistic and an individualistic meaning. Each person deserves the equal respect of all. At the same time, each person should be recognized as the source and the final judge of her own particular claims to happiness.

In this sense, the self-understanding of modernity is characterized not just by a theoretical "self-consciousness," by a self-critical attitude toward all tradition, but also by the moral and ethical ideals of "self-determination" and "self-realization." According to Hegel, this normative content of modernity has its seat in the structure of reason itself, and is explained by the "principle of subjectivity." Because Kant had already made a self-critical use of reason, and had developed the faculty of reason into a transcendental concept, Hegel could now read Kant's three Critiques as the definitive interpretation of the self-understanding of modernity. The *Critique of Pure Reason* explained the conditions for the possibility of an objectivating natural science, which frees the human mind from metaphysical illusions. The *Critique of Practical Reason* explained how persons, in conforming their wills to self-imposed laws through moral insight, thereby grant themselves autonomy. And the *Critique of Judgment* explained the necessary subjective conditions of an aesthetic experience that had become independent of any religious context.

Kant had distinguished practical reason and judgment from theoretical reason, but never relinquished the formal unity of the three faculties. At the end of the eighteenth century, these spheres of knowledge had also differentiated themselves from one another institutionally. In the spheres of science, morality, and art, questions of truth, of justice, and of good taste were discussed under differing aspects of validity, yet under the same discursive conditions of "criticism." Because Kant had explored the corresponding rational faculties as components of a transcendental subjectivity, Hegel had no hesitation in also regarding these cultural spheres of science and research, morality and law, and art and art criticism as "embodiments" of the principle of subjectivity. These objectifications offered themselves as objects of a critique of reason no less than the faculties themselves.

(3) We can now understand why the theme of "modernity" has retained such relevance for philosophy, and why philosophy has analyzed it from the perspective of a critique of reason. Moreover, the new time consciousness also explains the sort of "crisis" that the critical self-reassurance of modernity implies. "Critique and crisis"[6] becomes the model for philosophy's analysis because modern consciousness sees itself confronted with the challenge of solving problems that surge forth from an ever-widening horizon of possible, anticipated futures, toward an ever more disturbed and disturbing present. One thing above all is experienced as "critical": growing social complexity. This goes hand in hand with the differentiation and simultaneous de-traditionalization of a lifeworld as it dizzyingly loses the features of familiarity, transparency, and reliability that had once been able to absorb all contingencies. From this

defensive perspective, modernity is perceived as "inundating" the ethical life of a socially integrated form of life, and hence as a force of social disintegration.

Against this foil of "crisis and critique," Hegel could conceive of Kant's critique of reason as instructive but incomplete, and in this sense as a merely symptomatic effort to interpret the rational essence of the modern world. Hegel had to begin by deciphering the features of Kant's mirror image of modernity that remained hidden on the mirror's obverse side. Kant had succeeded in working out the very differentiations within reason that corresponded to the cultural spheres of science, morality, and art. But in Hegel's view he had not noticed the reverse side of these productive differentiations. What appeared as differentiations on the discursive level were experienced on the horizon of ethically integrated lifeworlds as just so many "diremptions" of an intuitive whole. Kant had misrecognized this painful abstraction just as much as the need for the recreation of a superseded totality at a higher stage. From this perspective, what had initially been celebrated as the principle of subjectivity, and the structures of self-consciousness posited with it, prove to be only a one-sided view of reason, which cannot be identical with reason as a whole. Certainly the activity of the understanding produces both subjective freedom and reflection, and is strong enough to undermine the power of religious tradition. Earlier, religion had essentially served as the guarantee of the ethical integration of social life, but the Enlightenment had shaken the foundations of religious life as such. And yet this fact only served to show that the principle of subjectivity is incapable of regenerating the unifying force of religion within the medium of reason. Religious orthodoxy, at the same time, in its mindless defensive battle against the abstractions of the Enlightenment, had decayed into a "positivity" that robbed religion of its binding force.[7]

In Hegel's view, then, the culture of the Enlightenment appeared as only the counterpart to a religion frozen into positivity. By putting reflection and instrumental rationality in the place of reason, the Enlightenment pursued an idolatry of reason; in this way the young Hegel discovered the same "positivism" in other areas of society and culture where the principle of subjectivity has also embedded itself – in empiricist science and abstract morality just as in romantic art, in the possessive individualism of bourgeois formal law and market economy, and in the instrumental politics of the great powers. The "positivity" of these alienating institutions and reified social relationships shows the principle of subjectivity to be a principle of repression, which now steps forth as the violence of reason itself. The repressive character of reason is grounded in the structure of self-reflection, i.e. in the self-reference of a knowing subject which makes itself into an object. The same subjectivity which had initially been the apparition – in the double sense of manifestation and illusion – of the source of all freedom and emancipation now reveals itself to be the origin of an objectification run wild. In the analytical force of reflection (an indispensable force, to be sure), Hegel also recognized a violence which, once set loose from the restraints of reason, objectified everything in its path, transforming all into possible objects of manipulation. Left to itself, "reflection" allowed dirempted organic wholes to collapse into their discrete parts. It dissolved intersubjective relationships into the reciprocally monitored action consequences of actors deciding on the basis of purposive rationality; isolated individuals were cut off from the roots of their common heritage. Hegel too of course depends on reflection. He moves in its medium in order to denounce the negativity of an understanding that has simply usurped the place of reason. Only through reflection can he demonstrate the limits of instrumental reason; only by completing an act of higher-stage reflection can he transcend its limits. Hence thought itself is, reflectively, pulled into the motion of the dialectic of Enlightenment. And it is only reason, in turn, that can give modernity – unprecedented, open to the future, anxious for novelty – its orientation.

Because modernity moves in a horizon open to the future, the completion of the dialectic of Enlightenment that Hegel had announced was, up to that point, nothing more than a bold promise. Hegel was well aware that the desired goal of reason forming itself into reality could only be proved with historical evidence. It is not the critical vision of modernity that separates the young Hegel from the mature Hegel; the problem, which I have sketched in necessarily simplified terms, is the same, but it was only the mature Hegel who dedicated himself to the completion of the program. He had to grasp both the antagonistic forms in which social disintegration appeared, and the historical developments and mechanisms through which the overcoming of these contrary tendencies, and the solution of these stubborn conflicts, became comprehensible. The *Philosophy of Right* was thus the attempt to conceptualize the ambivalent expressions of reason in society, i.e. in the social orders of family, market economy, and the nation-state. The social sphere – what we now call "society" – was revealed as a profoundly ambivalent spectrum of phenomena, and required a critical interpretation only from the perspective of a dialectic of Enlightenment.[8] On these grounds, philosophy became dependent on social theory, whose research program found its guidelines in philosophy, but was to be carried out with its own methods.[9]

II

I would now like to discuss, in three steps, the influential division of labor that was set up at the beginning of the twentieth century between philosophy and social theory, in the context of what Hegel understood as an analysis of the present. I would like (1) to recall briefly Max Weber's theory of social rationalization, which was dedicated to the interrogation of a "dialectic of Enlightenment." The aporetic consequences of older critical theory, which continued Max Weber's research program under the premises of Western Marxism, shows how this diagnosis led to a dead end (2). My radically simplified reconstruction characterizes the end of this theoretical development as coinciding with the end of the division of labor between philosophy and sociology. Rational choice theory and systems theory, respectively, appropriate the empirical explanatory claim of Weber's program; postmodernism, as it adopts the concepts of a critique of reason developed by Heidegger and Wittgenstein, carries this critique of modernity forward with different means. But these approaches encounter difficulties of their own (3). Postmodernism rejects the very criteria by which we can distinguish between the universalizing achievements of modernity and its colonizing features. The additional problem of the so-called incommensurability of language games and discourses, finally, will allow us to strike out on an alternative path in the last part of the lecture.

(1) Max Weber places European modernization in the context of a world-historical process of disenchantment.[10] Like Hegel, he begins with the transformation, and dissolution, of holistic religious worldviews as they lose their meaning-giving, orienting power. The rationalization of occidental culture results in the familiar differentiation between "value spheres." In the train of Rickert's neo-Kantianism, Weber proceeds on the assumption that each of these spheres – science, law and morality, art and art criticism – obeys its own logic in matters of fact, of justice, and of taste. Conflicts between these value spheres can no longer be rationally resolved from the higher standpoint of a religious or cosmological worldview. Nor can the unity of an intersubjectively shared worldview be replaced by the unifying force of theoretical or practical reason, in the name of objectivating science or rational morality.

Weber concentrates on the process of social modernization, a process driven forward by the administrative state and capitalist economy in tandem. The functional differentiation of state and economy produces an expansion of both an administrative apparatus dependent on taxation for its resources, and a market economy institutionalized via private law, and dependent on the framing conditions and infrastructures guaranteed by the state. Weber regards the institutional cores of state bureaucracies and organized businesses as the evolutionary achievements of social modernity, and the phenomena in need of explanation; they are, along with positive law, the pacemakers of social modernization. The explanation that Weber offers is reminiscent of Hegel. While Hegel had conceived of the significant structures of modern society as embodiments of a subject-centered reason, Weber understands social modernization as the institutionalization of instrumental-rational action, above all in the two core areas of state and economy.

For Weber, an organization counts as "rational" to the degree to which it enables – and obliges – its members to act in a purposive-rational manner. The two central organizations of modern society appear to meet this description: the modern institution of the state, on the one side, which implements a legally calculable, reliable, and efficient division of labor among well-trained, competent, and highly specialized officials; and, on the other side, capitalist enterprise, which sees to the economic allocation of productive forces and meets the pressures of competition and the labor market by raising labor productivity. In a nutshell, the bureaucratic state is tailored to the professionally competent, purposive-rational administrative conduct of civil servants, and the production modes of the market economy are tailored to the rational choices and the qualified labor power of managers and workers. Weber develops his famous argument of an affinity between Protestantism and the spirit of capitalism to explain the motivational basis of the elites who support these new institutions. But this historical starting point actually sets in motion a destructive developmental cycle, which Weber analyses as a frozen dialectic of Enlightenment.

The collapse of traditional worldviews, and the resulting rationalization of culture, lead to the widespread privatization of faith and an internalized ethics of conscience. The "Protestant ethic" in particular demands a rational conduct of life, and thus anchors purposive-rational modes of behavior through value-rational means. But in the course of ongoing modernization, the institutionalized rationality of these increasingly self-regulating economic and administrative systems frees itself from the motivational basis of religious value orientations. The new, legally constructed action spheres, which had first made possible the emancipation of the individual from the corporative collectives of premodern and early bourgeois civil society, now change into what Weber laments as an "iron cage." Marx had already derisively registered the ambivalence of the concept of "freedom" in the expression "free wage labor" – free from feudal bondage, but also free for the fate of exploitation, poverty, and unemployment that it meets in capitalism. In light of the growing complexity of independent action systems, Weber observes a similar broad transformation of freedoms into disciplines. On the basis of the disciplinary compulsions of bureaucratization and juridification, he paints a dark picture of an administered society.

In contrast to Hegel's diagnosis, the dialectic of Enlightenment here is interrupted, so to speak, and remains unfinished. Weber remains skeptical about the "charisma of reason." Without recourse to the motion of a totalizing reason, he sees no way to cope with social disintegration and to effect a transition to a less fragmented, more peaceful society. In his view, the "diremptions" produced by instrumental reason, permeating all of society, cannot be overcome from within society itself. Weber understands the "loss of freedom" and "loss of meaning" as existential challenges for individual persons. Beyond any futile hopes for redemption within the social order itself, only the absurd hope of a defiant individualism remains. Only the strong, self-reliant subject can, in lucky instances, succeed in forming a coherent life project of its own, in opposition to a rationalized, fragmented society. With the heroic courage of desperation, in the face of persistent and irresolvable social conflicts the resolute individual can realize freedom only privately, through her own personal life history.

This vision of an administered society is radicalized still further in the tradition of Western Marxism from Lukács to Adorno. From this perspective, hope in the strong individual's power of resistance now appears only as the residue of a vanished liberal epoch. Early critical theory appropriated the medium of analytical social psychology as a way of defending the assumption that dominant patterns of socialization transmit the functional imperatives of state and economy from the level of institutions to the level of personality structures.[11] The historical experiences of fascism and Stalinism confirmed the emerging picture of a totalitarian integration of society; a society that had long since broken the last resistance of heroic individuals imprisoned in their iron cage, and which can now be assured of the compliance of oversocialized subjects to its disciplinary matrices. The culture industry and mass media count as the most visible instruments of social control, while science and technology appear as the chief source of an instrumental rationality that penetrates all of society.

Horkheimer and Adorno's *Dialectic of Enlightenment* can be read as a re-translation of Weber's thesis into the language of the Hegelian-Marxist philosophy of history. It traces the origin of instrumental reason back to the instant where subjective mind and nature first split off from one another. On the other side, there is an obvious difference from Hegel too. For Hegel, the domination of reflection or the understanding remains only a moment within a totalizing, unifying reason. But for Horkheimer and Adorno subjective rationality, instrumentalizing both inner and outer nature as a whole, has ultimately usurped the place of reason, so that reason itself vanishes without a trace into "instrumental reason." This identification leaves instrumental reason with no intrinsic counterforce rooted within reason itself. A counteracting tendency to instrumental reason can be registered only in the dim remembrance of "mimetic" powers. Mimesis is Benjamin's and Adorno's name for the yearning lament of a dominated and violated nature, which is robbed of its own voice but can still find expression in the language of avant-garde art.

This leveling image of a totalizing modernity comprehensively screens out all of modernity's ambivalent features; Hegel's dialectic of Enlightenment is truncated. Worse still, while instrumental rationality is inflated into an unreasonable whole, the critique of this false whole is entangled in an aporia. As soon as the critique of instrumental reason can no longer be carried on in the name of reason itself, both it and the critique of modernity lose their normative foundation. Adorno constructed the virtue of a negative dialectics from the necessity of an aporia that a self-referential criticism has grown fully conscious of falling into. He remained faithful to the enterprise of a self-admittedly paradoxical, "groundless" critique, while he denied precisely those conditions that would have had to be fulfilled to make the business of exercising this critique *in actu* possible.

(2) This difficulty suggested that one part or another of the original project ought to be given up. One side, pursuing a theory of social modernity, abandons the philosophical idea of a self-critical self-reassurance of modernity, while the other side, exercising philosophical criticism, abandons the dialectic

of Enlightenment and the connection to social theory. The end of the cooperative division of labor between philosophy and social theory means uncoupling a critical self-understanding of modernity from an empirical observation and descriptive account of its tendencies to social crisis.

The descriptive approaches retain one basic premise from the classical conception of modernity: they proceed on the assumption that modern societies embody one type of rationality or another. This remains the case for the two currently most successful sociological approaches, rational choice theory and systems theory, each of which concentrates on one of the two rationality problematics that Weber had brilliantly conjoined – rational choice theory on the purposive rationality of individual actors, and systems theory on the functional rationality of large organizations. Within the confines of methodological individualism, rational choice theory attempts to explain patterns of interaction from the decisions of "rationally" acting subjects. Systems theory, on the other hand, provides a collectivist framework, reformulating what Weber had understood as organizational rationality into the functionalistic concepts of self-regulation, or autopoeisis. We thus acquire two competing pictures. For rational choice theory, modern societies are composed of loosely woven networks that arise from the interactions of countless, more or less rational agents. For systems theory, modern societies collapse into a multiplicity of independently operating, self-referential closed systems, which constitute environments for one another and can communicate with one another only indirectly, through mutual observation. The total absence of any intersubjectively shared values, norms, or processes of understanding makes both pictures resemble Weber's conception of the administered world in one aspect or another. Certainly, such features no longer count as indicators for the loss of freedom or meaning, or a lack of social integration. Indeed, descriptive theories leave no room for such evaluations; they only suggest an affirmative attitude toward modes of rationality insofar as their fundamental conceptions of rationality, which are constitutive for their respective choices of theoretical frameworks, are withdrawn from reflection and from all doubt.

A critical self-understanding of modernity requires a different approach. Heidegger and Wittgenstein offer alternative conceptions of reason, and new procedures for the critique of reason. Each, in his own way, succeeds in criticizing subject-centered reason without appealing to the totalizing power of Hegelian reason and its dialectic. Both address reason's destructive aspect, denouncing an instrumental reason gone wild. Once again, reason is equated with the operations of an objectifying and manipulating understanding, with "representational thinking" and philosophical abstraction, with the controlling power and discipline of a self-maintaining, narcissistically self-assertive subjectivity. But the constructive side of this critique appeals to a history of Being or a natural history, to an "Other of reason."

Although Heidegger's critique of science and technology, the exploitation of nature, mass culture, and other forms of expression of the totalizing age, shifts the accent from socioeconomic and political to cultural phenomena, this critique is nevertheless a counterpart to Western Marxism's critique of reification. In Germany, historicism and the philosophy of life had followed in the wake of the rise of the human sciences, shaking the assumption of the invariably transcendental features of the knowing subject. The mentalistic basic concepts of subjectivity and self-consciousness, rationality and reason, had already fallen victim to a sort of de-transcendentalization in Dilthey's time. With the turn from transcendental investigation to hermeneutics, the stage was set for a symbolically embodied, culturally contextualized, historically situated reason. The world-constituting spontaneity that had, until then, distinguished transcendental consciousness was carried over into symbolic forms (Cassirer), styles (Rothacker), worldviews (Jaspers), or systems of linguistic rules (Saussure).

Kant had conceived of reason as the faculty of ideas which expand the manifold of an endless multiplicity into a totality. On the one hand, ideas project the totality of possible appearances in space and time connected under causal laws. On the other hand, ideas also constitute a kingdom of ends, defined as the totality of intelligible beings subject only to self-legislated laws. With Hegel's critique of Kant, ideas also received the additional power of a self-reflective self-recuperation of their

own objectifications, and thus the power to consciously reinte-
grate an increasingly higher-level differentiation. Reason with a
capital "R" now gave the world process as a whole the structure
of a totality of totalities.

Heidegger, by contrast, reconstructs the history of metaphysics as the fateful sequence of epochal world disclosures,
which determine the limits of possible interpretations and practices in the world.[12] Ontologies are built into the syntax and
vocabulary of the predominant languages of each metaphysical
epoch. And these ontologies, in turn, determine the circumfer-
ence and the internal structures of the world, within which any
given linguistic community finds itself. Ontologies categorize
the holistic pre-understandings of members of linguistic communities, granting an a priori meaning to anything they can
encounter in the world. Subjects capable of speaking and acting
can observe events within their world, and can determine what
is relevant, and how events fit into pre-determined categories of
possible descriptions, only through the lenses of this pre-onto-
logical interpretation of the world, installed in deep grammar.
How members perceive something in the world, and how they
deal with it, depend on a linguistic world disclosure; from the
linguistic spotlight, so to speak, that illuminates everything that
can possibly occur in the world. This is an optical metaphor for
the framing effects of basic concepts, semantic connections,
relevances, and rationality standards. For each linguistic community, such grammatical structures in the broadest sense pre-
determine which expressions can count as well-formed,
meaningful, or valid. In regard to its world-disclosive function,
Heidegger conceives of language as an ensemble of enabling
conditions, which, while neither rational nor irrational in themselves, determine a priori what appears as rational or irrational
within their basic conceptual horizon.

In this respect Wittgenstein and Heidegger are more or less in
agreement – at least looked at retrospectively from the point of
view of a contexualism that highlights the convergences
between these two thinkers.[13] With his concept of language
games, Wittgenstein also focusses on the function of world
disclosure. On the basis of the internal relation between speaking and acting, the "grammar" of a language is also constitutive

for a corresponding practice or form of life. Wittgenstein and Heidegger both criticize the philosophical tradition, specifically metaphysics, for ignoring this dimension of linguistic world constitution. The rejection of this "Platonistic" error forms a common point of departure for what the two now understand – in an entirely new sense – as a critique of reason. For Heidegger, Plato and Platonism are guilty of the "forgetfulness of Being." They "forget" the meaning-giving background of the ontological pre-understanding that always shapes the historically specific roles of reason and rationality. According to Wittgenstein, the idealist tradition secures its basic concepts only by splitting linguistic practices off from the contexts in which practices find their proper place and "function." The metaphysical concepts of a self-sufficient reason, regarding itself as absolute insofar as it believes itself to be in control of its own conditions, arise from abstractive fallacies of this kind. For both Heidegger and Wittgenstein, the transcendental illusion of an unconditioned, pure, context-independent, and generalizing reason rises to a high point of delusion in the mentalistic paradigm. In contrast to Hegel, however, the critique of this subject-centered or instrumental reason can no longer naively rely on the speculative motion of self-reflection. The critique of reason thus transforms itself into a hermeneutics of suspicion, which seeks to reveal the Other of reason behind reason's own back. This genealogical path is the only way that an idolized subjectivity can be placed back into its historical context, a context that abstractive reason hides from itself in the form of its own unconscious.

Various postmodern theories appropriate this recontextualizing critique of reason in one version or another. Because they equate reason with the operations of the understanding, they preserve no remnants of the authority of earlier metaphysical concepts of an all-encompassing reason – not even in the form of a spur to recollection that torments Adorno as he testifies, in the last sentence of his *Negative Dialectics*, to his solidarity with a dethroned metaphysics "at the moment of its fall." Perhaps the masters did not see things in such an undifferentiated way as the pupils, who aim their postmodern critiques directly and unreservedly against the Enlightenment and its dialectic. Their critique of reason is meant not just to destroy the false image of an unconditioned and pure reason, but to rob the ideas of self-consciousness, self-determination, and self-realization of their normatively binding force. Not content in revealing the false pretensions of reason, these critiques seek to disempower reason as such. The attack on the "spirit of modernity" is intended to cure humanity of its preoccupation with the challenge of managing the pressure of too many problems coming from too much anticipation of too many future possibilities. The "locus of control" shifts from overburdened subjects to the fateful events of a history of Being, or to the contingent networks of a natural history or a language game.

(3) There can be no doubt concerning the healthy influence that postmodernism has had for contemporary debates. The critique of a form of reason that attributes a teleological design to history as a whole is just as convincing as the critiques of the ridiculous pretension of eliminating all social alienation. The emphasis on fragmentation, rupture, and marginalization, on otherness, difference, and the non-identical, as well as the regard for the particularities of the local and the individual, renew motives of early critical theory, above all of Benjamin. By strengthening the resistance to powers of abstract generalization and uniformization, postmodern critics take up Hegel's theme once again. But these welcome consequences arise from dubious premises, which, if correct, would exact an enormous cost. I would like to comment on two weaknesses: (a) a particular kind of linguistic idealism, and (b) the lack of understanding of the universalistic achievements of modernity.

(a) The recontextualizing critique of reason supports itself with an analysis of the world-disclosing function of language. This fact explains a certain tendency to overestimate the significance of grammars and vocabularies for the constitution of social infrastructures. Heidegger had already invested the texts and traditions of Western metaphysics, in the form of pre-established categorical frameworks or conceptual schemes, with the power to permeate and structure not just everyday experiences and interpretations, but the overall cultural and social practices of entire epochs. In this way, the backgrounded history of Western metaphysics was supposed to be reflected back in the foregrounded history of the world. A similar if less dramatic assimilation arises as Wittgenstein equates the structures of life forms with the grammars of language games. Unlike classical social theory, the concepts of ontologies and grammars now serve the exploration of patterns of interaction, institutional orders, and norms. From Marx to Durkheim and Max Weber, social facts had been analyzed under the categories of compulsion, exploitation and domination, forced sacrifice, and withheld satisfaction. The analytical strategy that Heidegger and Wittgenstein adopt traces the facticity of these limits back to more sublime forces: the selectivity of rules that determine the type and structure of philosophical texts and metaphysical traditions, literary styles, theoretical paradigms, and professional discourses. This displacement explains why postmodern research programs take up the tools of philological and aesthetic criticism, not of sociological critique.

While the classical conception of modernity was tailored to the experiences of social disintegration and the violation of universal norms, postmodern approaches direct their attention primarily to exclusions – to the exclusionary character of every unconsciously operating system of rules that is surreptitiously imposed on speakers and actors. Thus Foucault, for example, could write social and political history by using the concepts of a history of the discourse of the human sciences. Similarly, younger sociologists now write the history of modern societies in the concepts of a history of modern social theory – as if the material structure of society were made up of the concepts and discourses of social scientists.[14]

(b) The virtue of freeing reason from its false abstractions also forms a blind spot for the recontextualizing critique of reason. Postmodern approaches take every universalistic claim *per se* as a further sign of the imperialism of a disguised particularity pretending to stand for the whole. Since Marx, the test of this analytic strategy has been the unmasking of Eurocentric traditions and practices; the strategy articulates a general demand for the decentering of limited perspectives. The suspicion that mechanisms of exclusion are often embedded within the hidden presuppositions of universalistic discourses is well-founded – up to a point. But many postmodern theories lack a sufficient degree of sensitivity to the specific form of the discourse that arose with modernity, and that still distinguishes it. From the correct premise that there is no such thing as a context-transcendent reason, postmodernism draws the false conclusion that the criteria of reason themselves change with every new context.

It is not the claim to complete inclusion that distinguishes modern discourses from other kinds. The message of the world religions that emerged in the ancient empires was already addressed "to all," and was meant to accommodate all converts into the discourse of the faithful. What differentiates modern discourse, be it in science, morality, or law, is something else. These discourses are directed by principles, and submit themselves to self-reflective standards, in whose light factual violations of the injunction to complete inclusion can at once be discovered and criticized – for example, a hidden selectivity in the admission of possible participants, themes, or contributions. This recursive self-monitoring and self-correction explains the specific achievement of these principled, self-reflective discourses. To be sure, the self-referential structure and mode of operation of these discourses also gives rise to a particular form of discursive force, which is exercised in the mode of an occluded (because implicit) violation of the explicit promise of inclusion. But the mere fact that universalistic discourses are frequently misused as a medium for concealing social, political, epistemic and cultural violence is by itself no basis for renouncing the promise that is bound up with this discursive practice – all the less so since this practice provides both the criteria and the means for ensuring that the promise is kept.

Postmodern approaches rightly criticize the colonizing effects of the global domination of Western communicative patterns and discourses. This is true for a great part of the material and symbolic culture of Western civilization, which is disseminated through the global networks of markets and media. But such theories are poorly equipped for the task of distinguishing between colonizing discourses and convincing ones; between discourses that owe their global dissemination to systemic imperatives, and others that succeed on their own merits. Western science and technology are not just convincing and successful according to Western standards. And obviously human rights, despite ongoing cultural controversies over their correct interpretation, speak a language in which dissidents can express what they suffer, and what they demand from oppressive regimes – in Asia, South America, and Africa no less than in Europe and the United States.

III

As long as it is generated from the medium of a critique of reason, the diagnosis of modernity remains based on philosophical considerations. The classical conception of modernity, as we have seen, was developed under the premises of the philosophy of consciousness. After the linguistic turn, the mentalistic conception of a subject-centered reason was replaced by the detranscendentalized concept of a situated reason, setting the stage for a post-classical critique of modernity. But it is precisely this philosophical foundation that also presents postmodern theories with their characteristic difficulty. The assertion of an incommensurability of different paradigms and the "rationalities" peculiar to them is difficult to reconcile with the hypercritical attitude of postmodern theorists themselves. I will first (1) explore the problem of incommensurability and, taking a metacritical path, will justify a turn to a pragmatic conception of language. This pragmatic turn leads (2) to a concept of communicative reason, which provides a basis for a neoclassical reconceptualization of modernity. This diagnosis leads the way back, as I will show through the example of the theorem of reflexive modernization (3), to the division of labor between philosophy and social theory.

(1) A recontextualizing critique of reason is confined within the limits of an immanent critique, since it criticizes the false pretensions of pure reason only by pointing to the local background to which the supposedly unconditional standards of rationality in fact remain tied. We can only discover the

abstractive fallacy of a presumptive universalism if we unearth its concealed particularist roots. In this manner, postmodern approaches discover a multitude of traditions (MacIntyre) or discourses (Lyotard) which are constitutive for a worldview with its own standards of rationality. Each type of rationality marks a threshold we can only cross by performing a mental gestalt-switch. From the fixed perspective of a particular world-view, paradigm, life form, or culture, there is no hermeneutic transition to a next perspective. Since it is impossible to assume a "third," comparative standpoint, there can also be no transcendent criticism that would allow a transitive ordering of different rationalities on a scale of degrees of validity, or "semblances of truth." As soon as it becomes conscious of its own roots, a conception of rationality is just as acceptable as any other.[15]

And yet this way of looking at things still implicitly presupposes the image of a fragmented reason, whose shards are dispersed over many incommensurable – or partially overlapping – discourses. But if there is no such thing as a form of reason that can transcend its own context, then the philosopher who proposes this same picture may not lay claim to a perspective that allows him this overview. If the contextualist thesis is correct, then all are equally prohibited from gazing over the multitude of different discourses in which different, incommensurable types of rationality are supposed to be embodied. Under this premise, moreover, nobody can judge the validity of differing worldviews from the selective and hence prejudiced perspective of a particular, i.e. one's own, worldview. Foucault's "happy positivism" was meant to provide just such a fictional viewpoint beyond all selective viewpoints. To interrupt its own self-referentiality, a relativistic position must make an exception of the stated principle of incommensurability, precisely in the performative act of asserting it. This is why Rorty has suggested the sophisticated alternative of a "frank ethnocentrism." To the limiting cases of radical interpretation in the absence of any common language, Rorty applies the plausible notion that we normally understand expressions, and judge them to be either true or false, only in the light of our own standards. We should thus only be able to understand "their" views insofar as we can assimilate them, and the fundamental perspectives they are based on, into "our" views and our fundamental perspectives.[16] But this position neglects the hermeneutic insight into the symmetrical structure of every attempt to reach understanding;[17] it also cannot explain Rorty's paradoxical efforts to overcome a "Platonistic culture" in which (nearly) all of us are still imprisoned.

Clearly, something has gone wrong with a naturalization of reason that appeals to the linguistic constitution of self-referentially closed "worlds." An analysis that proceeds from the world-disclosing function of language emphasizes context-forming horizons that can be pushed further and further into the background but can never be transcended as such. If, on this view, linguistic analysis becomes entirely preoccupied with the question of how members of a linguistic community are guided in all that they do by an unavoidable, holistic pre-understanding of the world operating behind their backs, so to speak, then the very right to the communicative use of language falls by the wayside. The pragmatics of speech proceeds from the question of how communication participants – in the context of a shared lifeworld (or sufficiently overlapping lifeworlds) – can *achieve* an understanding about something in the world. This viewpoint moves entirely different phenomena into the foreground: the context-transcendent force of truth claims, for example, or of validity claims that speakers raise with their utterances in general; or the complementarity of first and second person perspectives; or the shared pragmatic presupposition that every agreement depends on the "yes" or "no" positions taken by the second person, so that both sides must be prepared to learn from one another, and so on. The symmetrical relations of the reciprocal recognition of communicative freedom and obligation offer an explanation beyond Davidson's "principle of charity" or Gadamer's insight into a "fusion of horizons" for the hermeneutical expectation that the gap between what initially appears as incommensurable can always, in principle, be bridged.

(2) I cannot go into the details of the communicative use of language or of communicative action here. In argumentation

and in everyday practice as well, communicative reason is always at work. Naturally, communicative reason too is embedded in the contexts of different forms of life. Each lifeworld provides its members with a common store of cultural knowledge, socialization patterns, values, and norms. The lifeworld can be thought of as the source of enabling conditions for communicative action, through whose medium, in turn, the lifeworld itself must be reproduced. But the symbolic structures of the lifeworld preserve an internal relation to communicative reason, which actors in their everyday practices must lay claim to as they raise criticizable validity claims and respond to them with a "yes" or a "no."

This explains the course of "rationalization" that lifeworlds undergo as they are pulled into the whirlpool of social modernization. The rationalization of a lifeworld, which is very different from "rationalizing" economic or administrative activities or their corresponding action systems, encompasses the three components of cultural traditions, socialization of individuals, and social integration.[18] Cultural traditions grow reflexive to the extent that they forfeit their taken-for-granted validity and open themselves up to criticism. The continuity of tradition thenceforth demands its conscious appropriation by succeeding generations. At the same time, socialization processes increasingly tend to foster formal competencies; cognitive structures that break loose from concrete contents. Persons are increasingly furnished with an abstract self-identity. Capacities for a postconventional mode of self-regulation are the response to the social expectations of autonomous decisions and individualized life projects. The processes of social integration are increasingly uncoupled from established traditions. On the level of institutions, general moral principles and procedures replace concrete, inherited values and norms. And the political regulation of collective life is increasingly dependent on the deliberative bodies of constitutional states, as well as the communicative processes of civil society and political public spheres.

This rough sketch can serve as the basis for a reformulation of the basic features of Weber's diagnosis. At first, a certain rationalization of premodern lifeworlds fulfilled the cognitive and motivational initial conditions for a capitalist form of economy and an administrative state. In their course of development, these two functionally integrated action systems transformed themselves into self-regulating systems steered by money and administrative power. Their dynamic gained a certain independence from the action orientations and attitudes of individual and collective actors. For the actors, higher levels of system differentiation bring the advantage of a higher level of freedom. But the advantage of an expanded range of options goes hand in hand with social uprooting, and with a new sort of compulsion imposed on actors by the contingent ups and downs of economic cycles, by the disciplining of labor, by unemployment, by uniform bureaucratic regulations, ideological conditioning, political mobilization, and so on. The balance of these very mixed results tips to the negative the moment that the economic and administrative subsystems spill over into the lifeworld's core areas of cultural reproduction, socialization, and social integration. Of course, the economic system and the state apparatus must for their part be legally institutionalized in the contexts of the lifeworld. But alienation effects increasingly emerge when spheres of life that are functionally dependent on value orientations, binding norms, and processes of understanding are monetarized and bureaucratized. Weber had diagnosed social pathologies of this sort as loss of meaning and loss of freedom.

The classical conception of modernity as developed by Weber, Lukács, and the early Frankfurt School was based upon the abstract opposition between a disciplinary society and the fragile subjectivity of individuals. With the transition to an intersubjectivist model, this confrontation is replaced by circular processes between lifeworlds and systems. This allows a greater sensibility for the ambiguity of social modernization. Growing social complexity does not *per se* generate alienation effects. It can just as well expand the range of options and learning capacities – provided the division of labor between system and lifeworld remains intact, at any rate. Social pathologies[19] arise only as a consequence of an invasion by exchange relations and bureaucratic regulation of the communicative core areas of the private and public spheres of the lifeworld.

These pathologies are not limited to personality structures; they extend just as much to the transmission of meaning and the dynamic of social integration. This interaction between system and lifeworld is reflected in the imbalanced division of labor between the three forces that hold society together: solidarity, on the one side; money and administrative power on the other.

(3) This proposed reformulation also permits an answer to the problem posed today in the form of "reflexive modernization."[20] Normally, members of a lifeworld draw solidarity from inherited values and norms, and from established and standardized communicative patterns. In the course of the rationalization of the lifeworld, however, this ascriptive background consensus shrinks, or shatters. It has to be replaced by the interpretive accomplishments of communication participants themselves. This circumstance brings me to the contemporary situation. Rationalized lifeworlds, with their institutionalized discourses, have access to their own mechanism for generating new bonds and normative arrangements. In the sphere of the lifeworld, "rationalization" does not plug the wellsprings of solidarity; rather, it discovers new ones as the old ones run dry. This productive force of communication is also significant for the challenge of "reflexive modernization."

This theory places familiar "postindustrial developments" in a specific light – the collapse of social differentiations along traditional class- and gender-based lines, the loosening up of standardized mass production and mass consumption, the disruption of stable commercial and security systems, the increased flexibility of large-scale organizations, labor markets, party affiliations, etc. Postindustrial societies have expended all the reserves that had fueled "simple" industrialization – preexisting natural resources, as well as the cultural and social capital of premodern social formations. At the same time, postindustrial societies encounter the consequences of social reproduction, which appear in the form of systemically generated risks that can no longer be externalized, i.e. shifted onto foreign societies or cultures, to other social sectors, or to future generations. Hence modern societies collide with their own limits in a double sense: they become "reflexive" insofar as they perceive this situation as such and react to it. Because they are less and less able to reach back to traditions, or external resources like nature, they must increasingly reproduce on their own all the provisions for their continuing existence. The modernization of "halfway-modern" societies that Ulrich Beck refers to[21] succeeds only "reflexively," insofar as these societies are obliged to fall back on their own resources to deal with the problems arising from social modernization.

Of course, "reflexivity" can be understood both in the sense of a "self-application" of systemic mechanisms, as well as in the sense of a "self-reflection," i.e. the self-perception and self-effectuation of collective actors. An example of reflexivity in this first sense is the market economy's absorption of market economy-generated environmental pollution. An example of self-reflection would be efforts to bring global markets under control by influencing their structural conditions through a "world domestic policy." Because the functional differentiation of highly specialized subsystems is always "ongoing," systems theory assumes that systems will be able to correct themselves through reflexive mechanisms. But this expectation must not be overblown: social subsystems, which speak only in their own languages, are deaf to the external effects they produce. Markets can only react to "costs" that are expressed through price. The cost of conflicting system rationalities can obviously only be kept within socially tolerable limits with a reflexivity of the other, second sort; through self-reflection in the sense of political self-direction and self-realization. Ongoing modernity must be carried on with political will and awareness. And for this form of democratic self-direction, the construction of procedures of discursive opinion- and will-formation is crucial.[22]

Not just the political will-formation of citizens but also the private lives of members of society depend on the source of discursively generated solidarity. As standardized living conditions and career patterns dissolve, and options multiply, individuals come to feel the increasing weight of decisions and arrangements that they now have to make by themselves. The drive toward "individualization" demands the discovery and the construction of new social regulations. Liberated subjects, no longer bound and directed by traditional roles, have to fashion new commitments by the force of their own communicative efforts alone.[23]

These hasty remarks are only meant to indicate how the communicative theoretical approach leads back to a neoclassical conception of modernity, which in turn relies on the support of a critical social theory. But philosophical lenses now demand a stereoscopic view of the ambivalence of modernity. The analysis must keep in mind both the emancipating, unburdening effects of a communicative rationalization of the lifeworld, and the effects of a functionalistic reason run wild.

7

The Differing Rhythms of Philosophy and Politics

Herbert Marcuse at 100 ·

Following the death of his first wife, Sophie, Herbert Marcuse wrote to Horkheimer and Pollock on March 3, 1951: "The idea that death is a part of life is false, and we should take much more seriously Horkheimer's notion that it is only with the elimination of death that humanity could be truly happy and free." Eternal life in the here and now – Marcuse appropriated a vitalistic version of this profoundly un-Protestant conception, which goes back to Condorcet. Despite all the progress in gene technology, it has, so far, yet to be realized. Otherwise Marcuse might still be alive to witness the peculiar connection between his own 100th birthday and another anniversary: "1989–1968–1998" was the theme of a memorial conference for Marcuse held a few weeks ago in Genoa. Scholars and other friends of philosophy attended. But only the retrospective on Marcuse's disputed role as a mentor of the student revolts of 1968 provoked the audience's intense interest. It is as if the coincidence of his centenary with the 30th anniversary of the events of 1968 protects Marcuse from being forgotten, far more than the lingering echoes of his philosophical work.

The dwindling effects of a once widely read body of work can often be merely a symptom of the temporary depletion of an overly rich influence. This was the case with Adorno, whose work has, rightly, remained a challenge for the present. Even

Published in *Neue Zürcher Zeitung*, July 18–19, 1998.

Horkheimer's work continues to be of interest in the context of
the school that he inspired. But in Herbert Marcuse's case, the
image of the scholarly writer fades behind the image of Marcuse
the political writer and instigator. We are all familiar with the
particular ups and downs in the reception of important, or less
important, philosophers. The aftereffects of political interventions, which are much more closely bound up with their contemporary historical context than philosophical works, are
subject to different, shorter rhythms. In Marcuse's case, there
seems to have been a kind of short-circuit between the rhythms
of the history of the influence of the work, and those of the
political figure. As the political engagement is devalued, the
weight of the philosophical teaching seems to be pulled into its
wake. This suggests advocating the latter at the expense of the
former. But if something like this is my goal here, then we
should be aware of the dangers of an optical distortion in both
directions – in respect of the political engagement, no less than
in respect of philosophy.

Compared with other members of the small circle around
Horkheimer, Marcuse was surely the one genuine political
temperament. In 1918 he was a member of a Berlin soldiers'
council; sixty years later he still described his disappointment
over the "failure of the German revolution which my friends
and I...experienced with the murders of Karl and Rosa."
During the Second World War, Marcuse worked in the political
section of the Office of Strategic Services; preparing "enemy
analyses" was a way of participating, in his own way, in the
battle against the regime that had driven him from Germany. In
the early 1960s he was repoliticized by the American civil rights
movement; he subsequently took part in the opposition to the
war in Vietnam and finally became an influential voice in the
student protest movements on both sides of the Atlantic. Of
course, this occasional activism shouldn't conceal the fact that
Marcuse, even in comparison with Horkheimer and Adorno,
was in a strict sense an academic figure, who conformed to the
rules of the profession and produced scholarly books.

Under Heidegger's tuition, Marcuse had become familiar
with the issues and the standards of contemporary philosophy.
The first "Heideggerian Marxist" wrote his *Habilitation* in a

conventional style, and in 1930 published works in leading academic journals. It was Marcuse, not Adorno, who assumed the role of philosopher in the division of labor that Horkheimer had laid down for the Institute for Social Research in New York, and it was Marcuse who wrote the commentary for Horkheimer's seminal essay on "Traditional and Critical Theory." In 1941, Marcuse received well-deserved recognition, even within the discipline of philosophy, for his systematic historical investigation of the emergence of social theory from Hegel's philosophy. *Reason and Revolution* holds up to every comparison with Karl Löwith's famous counterpiece, *From Hegel to Nietzsche*. Marcuse even regarded *Eros and Civilization*, his most radical and in a sense his most distinctively "Marcusean" book, as a contribution to a disciplinary discussion. *One Dimensional Man* is the best-known book; it is not the best. It appeared in 1964 and ends, with deep pessimism, with the quote from Benjamin that "only for the sake of the hopeless is hope given to us" – entirely without that "connection to praxis" that his students immediately constructed.

In his preface to *Reason and Revolution*, Marcuse grounds his study of Hegel with the claim that "the rise of fascism calls for a reinterpretation of Hegel's philosophy." If it is true that Marcuse's work has fallen into the shadows of a past political reality, then we will have to draw a new lesson from it for a changed historical situation. It is not that we must see his philosophy "in a new light"; rather, we must examine our own biases concerning the political role of the author.

Wolfgang Kraushaar's painstaking documentation of *The Frankfurt School and the Student Movement* confirms the direct influence Marcuse had for the 1968 student movement in the Federal Republic of Germany. Important motifs are already audible in a speech that Marcuse delivered on May 22, 1966 for a conference on Vietnam organized by Students for a Democratic Society (SDS) at Frankfurt University. Marcuse speaks of "the contrast between social wealth, technological progress, and the domination of nature on the one hand, and on the other hand the use of all these forces for the perpetuation of the struggle for existence on the national and global level... in the face of poverty and misery." Today, after the

end of the arms race between the superpowers, the "destructive use of accumulated wealth" is surely less glaring than at the
time of the Vietnam War. But under the flag of global capitalism, which raises both unemployment figures and the stock
markets at the same tempo, Marcuse's central assertion of a
"fatal unity of productivity and destructiveness" is confirmed in
other, no less drastic, ways.

Marcuse understood that productive forces have been freed
from existing relations of production, rather than chained to
them. He questioned the productivist model of social emancipation. Long before the Club of Rome, he struggled against "the
horrible concept of progressive productivity, for which nature is
simply there, gratis, to be exploited." In the meantime ecology
movements have brought this issue to the awareness of the
general public. Marcuse looked for the difference between socialism and capitalism "not so much in the development of
productive forces, as in their reversal. This is the presupposition
for the elimination of labor, the autonomy of needs, and the
pacification of the struggle for existence." In light of the thesis of
the "end of the labor-based society," even claims such as these
appear plausible. According to one widely disseminated esti-
mate, the total social product of all the OECD countries could
be produced by 20 percent of the working population. But if
greater numbers of the working population become "superfluous" for social reproduction, the tight connection between successful work and social recognition can hardly survive.

Even Marcuse's appraisal of the potential for protest is by no
means unrealistic. He did not see the Soviet Union as a counterforce to the capitalist West. Nor did he share the view that
society's generalizable interests are only expressed in the suffering and resistance of the exploited masses. In the United States,
another kind of minority–majority relationship was already
becoming visible. A cohesive majority stood opposed to a marginalized minority which had ability to threaten it. Marcuse
thus placed his hope in the moral sensibilities of youth, intellectuals, women, religious groups, etc. The driving force of
the normative had to be brought to bear in the material
interests of the downtrodden and oppressed: "One of the
things I have learned... is that morality and ethics are not

mere superstructure, and are not just ideology." Marcuse spoke quite idealistically of the "solidarity of reason and sentiment." As sociologists establish the transformation that has taken place from material to so-called postmaterial value orientations, even this notion gains a degree of plausibility.

Of course, these arguments do not really explain the broad resonance that Marcuse found among his student readers. It was the impulse of a philosophy of life, tinged with Freudianism, that secured Marcuse's wide influence for the grandchildren's generation. Marcuse, who himself had been molded by the German youth movement at the turn of the century, had a sense of the culturally revolutionary character of the new youth movement – the impulse for revolt, and the self-understanding of the rebellious: "This opposition is . . . sexual, moral, intellectual, and political rebellion in one. In that sense, it is total, directed at the system as a whole."

This last formulation surely also betrays how this existentialist description invites the connection between youth revolt and a conception of the total transformation of the whole, the concept of "revolution," borrowed from the philosophy of history. Marcuse himself certainly never confused revolt and revolution; but he had full faith in the role of revolt as revolution's igniting spark. He suggested to his listeners that they should understand themselves as a part of the coming revolutionary movement. This also explains his ambiguous comments on the question of the use of violence. In Berlin in July 1967, Marcuse already distanced himself from the liberal wing of the SDS with a remark directed at Knut Nevermann: "I have in no way equated humanity with nonviolence. On the contrary, I have spoken of situations where a transition to violence is precisely in the interest of humanity." This tendency was sponsored by a radical-authoritarian and intellectual-elitist understanding of philosophy and Enlightenment that Marcuse, together with others of his generation, owed to the politically dubious curriculum of the German *Gymnasium*. Even Hannah Arendt was not entirely distanced from it.

The illusory equation of rebellious youth with a revolutionary vanguard may explain, in part, the rather attenuated influence of Marcuse the philosopher. The false actualization of the events of 1968 make it difficult today, in hindsight, to divorce the achievements of the academic scholar from the never-arrived *kairos*, the historical context that lifted Marcuse's status to that of a falsifying authority. It would not be the first time that a philosophy perishes from the very history that it had itself elevated to the final criterion of *verum* and *falsum*. Of course, the malicious tone of this judgment is undeserved. It does not do justice to the truth content that Marcuse's analysis also possesses. Marcuse grasped the particular entwinement of the productivity of economic growth and the destructiveness of its social consequences, but he did so with the sort of spellbinding, totalizing concepts that have grown strange to us. He built his diagnosis up into a vision of a totalitarian, closed society because he believed he had to introduce a vocabulary that could only open clouded eyes to phenomena that had grown invisible, by bathing apparently familiar phenomena in a harsh counterlight.

This situation has changed. Nobody who reads the newspapers today can be deceived about the entwinement of productivity and destructiveness. High-intensity "locational competition" has plunged our governments into a cost-cutting deregulatory frenzy which over the last decade has generated obscene profits and drastic income disparities, the devastation of cultural infrastructures, rising unemployment, and the marginalization of a growing population of the poor. We do not need a new language to recognize this, because we no longer imagine ourselves to be living in an "affluent society."

The intellectual situation has changed as well. Postmodernism has disarmed modernity of its self-understanding. We can no longer tell whether the democratic conception of a society that realizes itself through the will and consciousness of its united citizens has come to resemble an endearingly old-fashioned utopia, or a dangerous one. In league with a pessimistic anthropology, neoliberalism makes us daily more familiar with a new world order where social inequities and exclusions count as facts of nature once more. Existing constitutions suggest an entirely different way of seeing things. Perhaps we still need a renovated language if this normative way of looking at things, as opposed to the demands for adaptation to functional imperatives, is not to be completely forgotten.

8

An Argument against Human Cloning
Three Replies

Elisabeth Beck-Gernsheim convincingly describes the process that takes place as new genetic medical technologies are introduced to the public: initial moral indignation, followed by normalization.[1] It is not just the interest of researchers in their own reputations, nor just the interest of manufacturers in their own economic success that clears the way for new innovations. New products clearly also satisfy the interest of consumers. And this interest is often compelling enough to make moral considerations fade over the course of time. Isn't the reduction of suffering also a moral argument?

This is the threshold where empirical facts and normative considerations meet. The normalization of these new technologies presumably doesn't take place under the pressure of growing demand alone. The weaker the moral objections that hold them in check – the desire for one's own child, for example – the faster scientific, commercial, and consumer interests will win out. But in the case of human cloning, its seems to me that a weighty normative argument does come into play. There is a rational kernel to the archaic revulsion provoked by the vision of cloned human replicas.

The genetic material of a newborn child has, until now, been understood in terms of "fate," or as a purely contingent circumstance, as the product of an accidental process that the growing

Published in *Süddeutsche Zeitung*, January 17–18, 1998.

person lives with, and that she has to find her own responses to. The grammatical ambiguity in the basic ethical question of who we are, and who we would like to be, can indeed be explained by the fact that, in a certain sense, we already find ourselves to be a particular person. We are responsible for our acts and our omissions, even though we have no access to a fundamental store of traits, aptitudes, or inherited characteristics.

Some understand this as the "fate" that we must assume; others see it as the challenge "to become who one wants to be." We can understand this contingency either in a religious or in a postmetaphysical sense. In either case, there is one condition that remains essential if we are to bear the burden of responsibility for our actions: No person may so dispose over another person, may so control his possibilities for acting, in such a way that the dependent person is deprived of an essential part of his freedom. This condition is violated if one person decides the genetic makeup of another. In the process of self-understanding, the clone also encounters himself as a particular person; but behind the core stock of these traits, aptitudes, and characteristics stand the intentions of a stranger.

This fact distinguishes the case of a deliberately cloned person from that of identical twins. The problem is one of presumptuousness and servitude, not the identity of two organisms that have grown from a single cell. This technology constructs a new decision competence that is comparable with the historical example of slavery. Slavery is a legal relationship signifying that one person disposes over another as property. It therefore cannot be harmonized with the currently valid concepts of constitutional law: human rights and human dignity.

According to the same moral criteria, then, and not merely on religious grounds, the copying of the genetic material of a human being must be condemned. This procedure destroys an essential presupposition of responsible action. Of course, we have been dependent on our genetic makeups until now. But we cannot hold any accountable person to be liable for such a makeup itself. The clone is comparable to a slave insofar as he can shift a portion of the responsibility for his actions, which he would otherwise have to bear entirely by himself, onto other persons. For the clone, that is, a judgement that another person has passed upon him prior to his birth hardens into an irreversible code.

Moreover, the slave owner robs himself of his own freedom at the same time as he deprives another person of his. Within a democratic legal order, citizens can only enjoy equal private and public autonomy if all of them mutually acknowledge one another's autonomy. A person who sets himself up as master over the genetic material of another revokes this fundamental reciprocity. The matter has its obscene side for the one whose genetic program is reproduced: can he really regard himself as so perfect that he could want an exact copy of all his own traits and characteristics?

Certainly, the comparison with slavery also falls short. The emancipation of slaves would indeed correspond with an emancipation not from a genetic code, but from the deliberate reproduction of this code by someone else. Moreover, a life history is the only medium in which persons can form their irreplaceable identity. The genetic code is not irrevocable in the sense that it fixes the identity of a person in the way that a master fixes the social status of a slave; otherwise the assumption of responsible action in general would be rendered meaningless. While we all have to live with the determinations, talents, and handicaps of a genetic code, what matters from the perspective of the actor herself is how we ourselves respond to these facts, how we deal with what we understand as the givens of our own birth.

This doesn't make the problem disappear. For a clone, such "givens" are no longer accidental circumstances. What others can accept as something that just "happens," he has to calculate as the results of the actions of another person. And it is precisely this changed perspective which, if I am seeing it correctly, has to reach deeply into our moral self-understanding, because it violates the reciprocity between those born equal.

The question of whether a society ought to refrain from doing something that it has the power to do quickly becomes a question of rights. Elisabeth Beck-Gernsheim mentions an article by a well-known American jurist in favor of permitting human cloning, which introduces the argument that the production of cloned human beings should not be met with legal obstacles, since any preventive legal discrimination would in fact lead to the marginalization of a new minority group. Clones would be even more badly "marked" than other minorities. As I read this article by Lawrence Tribe in the *New York Times* at the beginning of December, I was initially impressed. The liberal argument – as distinguished from the pressures of the market-liberal side – does indeed have a normatively convincing force. On the other hand, it ought to make us reflect on two things.

Before we scrutinize the way that we might see cloned human beings, we would have to ask how they would see themselves – and whether it is a view that we ought to impose on them. Second, the premise itself is dubious. This is also my question to the sociologists: Is the normalization of new technologies which initially provoke our moral indignation unavoidable in this case of homunculi reproduced by genetic technology? Or can moral reasons, if publicly convincing, not also have an empirical effect?

Nature Does not Forbid Cloning: We Must Decide for Ourselves[2]

On the question of permitting human cloning, Dieter E. Zimmer argues that we should not let ourselves be guided by moral categories such as freedom and responsibility, but rather by biology.[3] Any rational discussion of bioethical questions surely requires an adequate familiarity with the ongoing scientific developments and relevant scientific facts. But normative questions cannot be reasonably discussed without reference to a normative point of view.

Zimmer himself opposes the cloning of human organisms, arguing that cloning would arrest the accident-steered combination of parental genes that serves as a natural mechanism for genetic variation. It is precisely this mechanism that brings newborns into the world as genetically unique beings – with the statistically insignificant exception of identical twins. Because humanity – understood as a "species being" – owes its "adaptive genius" to the broad variation of traits, Zimmer concludes, "if human beings were to begin cloning themselves, they would collide with one of the principles to which they owe their existence. Therefore they ought not to allow it." Of course, this reflection only becomes a practical conclusion if we attach normative assumptions to it. Either Zimmer regards our species-specific "adaptive capacity" *per se* as a value that should be optimized, or he shows that such an optimization on this scale is still necessary for the preservation of the species, even under given civilized conditions, and then expands this purely empirical determination with the moral injunction that we have a duty to preserve the species, and hence to continue human life by reproduction. Do we have such a duty?

Biology cannot relieve us of moral reflection. And bioethics should not provide us with biologistic detours around it. On the other hand, normative points of view are contested; and all the more so in cases of the moral inclusion of new phenomena. This is naturally also the case with the efforts to use Kantian concepts to come to terms with the possible consequences of the cloning of human organisms.

I proceed on the assumption that the universalistic principles of an egalitarian legal order permit only those decision competencies that are capable of harmonizing with the mutual respect for the equal autonomy of each citizen. Thus, for example, another person may have a spatially and temporally limited disposal over my own labor power only if I have given my consent. Of course many "particular relations of force" obtain, for example between parents and children. Notwithstanding the fact that parental force is itself legally limited, the question of whether human cloning would impinge on the fundamental symmetry of mutual relations between free and equal legal persons only requires that we regard the relations of mature or adult persons in the legal sense. The dependence on the fate of socialization, in any event, is of another kind entirely than genetic fate: the maturing person can, in given situations, "turn her back" on the parental home and "break" with its traditions, while remaining in a certain sense consigned to her own genes.

The question is how the moral self-understanding of an adult person would change if that person is not, as we say, naturally produced, but has been cloned. Obviously, the fact of dependence on a genetic program has not altered; rather, what is new is the dependence on the deliberate fixing of this program by another person. If parents decide to have their own child, the accident-steered combination of genes from both parents produces an unpredictable genealogical situation. Zimmer correctly emphasizes the difference between this decision, and the decision of a single person to construct an exact copy of his own genetic code; thus in a sense an exact copy of himself. This would introduce a previously unknown form of interpersonal relationship between genetic original and genetic copy. The intentional fixing of inherited genetic material means that the clone has been placed under a lifelong judgment imposed by another. Whoever does not care for the connotations of this juridical metaphor can, like Lutz Wingert, speak of an interpersonal relationship that has become like the relation between a product and its designer.

Be that as it may, a problem exists for both sides: the moral obscenity of an autocratic, self-absorbed duplication of one's own genetic makeup on the side of the reproducer; and on the side of the reproduced clone, the problem that someone has entered into a zone that otherwise no other person has any access to. Of course, the cloned person would have the same freedom as anybody else in the course of a reflexively appropriated and voluntarily led life history; the freedom to relate to her own talents and handicaps and to find constructive responses to the circumstances surrounding her beginning. But for her, these "givens of birth," or whatever she takes them to be, at any rate, are no longer accidental circumstances but are the results of a deliberate act. The clone can ascribe to another person's intention what in every other case remains a contingent event. This ascription of an intentional intervention into an otherwise inaccessible zone constitutes the morally and legally relevant difference.

The expression "inaccessible" should only mean: removed from the grasp of another person with whom we are, normatively regarded, on an equal footing. Obviously the modern understanding of freedom of action entails that the conditions for the development of personal identity, in this sense, are inaccessible. If not, the mutual recognition of equal freedom for all is called into question. The clone knows that he could not make the same sorts of arrangements for his producer as his producer made for him; not just contingently, but in principle. One might object against this that children created by their parents also could not, conversely, create their parents. But this asymmetry essentially relates to the circumstance that the child has come into the world at all; i.e. the sheer fact of her existence, and not the mode and the manner in which the child can lead this existence on the basis of an inherited store of capabilities and characteristics.

I am not sure how this change of perspective would affect our moral self-understanding. As far as I can see, human cloning would injure the conditions of symmetry in the relations of adult persons to one another, on which the idea of mutual respect under equal freedom has been based until now.

But this conclusion does not extend, as Zimmer maintains, to any number of therapeutic interventions into the organism of a dependent who is not asked, not even for the preventive elimination of diseases (which of course can be permitted but never dictated). I see exclusively negative arguments for a normative justification of such well-circumscribed genetic-technological interventions, in general the avoidance of evils. Perhaps that is already too weak a formulation, since the definition of "evils" depends on cultural criteria that can be very problematic. Didn't "inferior races" once count as an evil? I don't have the impression that we have arrived at the right answers to the moral and legal questions of genetic technology and reproductive medicine. But biology alone cannot give them to us.

The Cloned Person would not be an Injury to Civil Rights[4]

I admire the interventions of Reinhard Merkel, even if I am not entirely convinced by them.[5] What is not in dispute – unlike in my disagreement with Dieter E. Zimmer – is the value of moral and legal arguments or the weight that they assume in relation to biological and sociological factors. It is only the mode of normative arguments themselves that is in dispute between us. From the empirical perspective that Merkel favors, no "harm" is inflicted on a cloned human being. But anybody who favors a Kantian reading of the categories of "freedom" and "responsibility" will have reservations about the unprecedented decision competence that this new procedure would introduce. I regard the debate among philosophers as neither idle nor undecidable. Here too, theories have to fit the phenomena.

The main issue is the question of what the significance is for a person – whether it makes a morally relevant difference for her self-understanding – "in what manner she has come to receive her own genome": through accident, or through a determined or arbitrary act. In order to bring the right phenomena into focus, we have to assume the perspective of an actor who wishes to know who he is and how he should live his life. He will thus have to relate in one way or another to his genetic makeup, or what he regards as the givens of his birth. From the perspective of an ethical self-understanding, one's genome certainly fixes the conditions for identity formation. But we interpret these predispositions as in part enabling, and in part limiting conditions. We identify ourselves with our talents more than with our handicaps. And we can understand this, in turn, as a challenge, rather than a "crippling" fate. How a self-understanding develops depends among other things on interpretive patterns that predominate within a culture.

It obviously makes a difference whether we conceive of this genetic makeup as the result of an accidental natural process, or as a part of a "hidden" plan, or as religious grace, as the will of God. Interpretations such as these mold the consciousness of freedom with which persons will perform their routine actions. But how could this consciousness remain untouched by the knowledge that the design of one's own genome was carried out neither by the chance of nature, nor by the provision of God, but by a peer?

The arbitrary disposition over the genetic makeup of another person would introduce a previously unknown relationship between producer and produced, between genetic copy and original. This relation of dependency deviates from all known interpersonal relationships insofar as it fundamentally resists being transformed into a relation of equals, between normatively equal partners deserving of equal treatment. The designer fixes the initial shape of his product irrevocably and asymmetrically – without any possibility for a change of roles.

Reinhard Merkel merely evades the problem when he compares a person who is "mentally handicapped due to a genetic defect" with a healthy person, and argues: "Which possibilities for freedom and responsibility one is biologically disposed to at the beginning of one's existence depends solely on the composition of one's genome, not on how, or from whom, one has got it." The difference that I am concerned with doesn't consist in the composition of inherited predispositions; it consists in the moral self-understanding that must change as soon as the affected person ascribes the decision over the natural bases of her own development to someone else, because she encounters a foreign intention in the mirror image of her own predispositions.

Merkels' two further objections also shift the problem onto another level. With the thought experiment of the duplication of a human embryo at an early stage, Merkel distracts himself from the heart of the matter, since in this case the decisive aspect of the deliberate creation of a copy of a known genetic original is missing. Whatever one could say about this case, my own reservations are directed against the duplication of the genome of a mature human organism, not against the biological procedure of cloning as such. Indeed the current discussion was touched off by the news of the cloned sheep Dolly and the macabre futural fantasies that this event provoked.

Finally, Merkel objects that the producer cannot commit any legal harm against the cloned person, since the cloned person owes his existence only to this questionable act: "This is why no 'symmetrical conditions of mutual respect' could have been injured in relation to the clone, because the act to which he owes his very existence is, for him, in no sense qualifiable as an injury." An attorney might argue in this way in the case of an infringement of civil rights that has already taken place. But if we want to speak juridically, our discussion deals with a question of constitutional law: Whether a type of constructive procedure should be allowed that introduces (if my analysis is correct) an unprecedented decision competence, and that injures a necessary presupposition for the normative equality of all legal persons.

A variety of metaphors is in circulation to describe this injury. We talk of designers who manufacture a product, or of a judge passing a final judgment – an image that religious sensibilities still come closest to. These metaphors are nearly as inadequate as that of the slave owner who mistakes persons for things – they all allude to the decision situations between simultaneously acting persons. They ignore the distance between the present and an irreversible past; between a decision made before birth and the subsequent life history whose entire course this decision will affect. Isn't what is most disturbing precisely the aspect for which the right image is lacking? I am thinking of the constant, irreversible effects of the arbitrary decision of another person on "me" – not insofar as I exist at all, but rather on the essential conditions of my self-understanding.

Notes

Foreword

1 It is not conceit that leads me to reprint my controversial speech on Goldhagen (which first appeared in K.D. Bredthauer and A. Heinrich (eds), *Aus der Geschichte lernen*, Edition Blätter 2, Bonn 1997, 14–37). Indeed I have no doubts concerning the professional competence of the historians critical of Goldhagen. But I do regret that the issue that was announced in the title of that speech vanished in the course of the controversy itself – I mean the necessary differentiations in the public uses of history. These differentiations decay into a demagogic politics of history if we do not carefully distinguish between the moral position toward, the juridical treatment of, and the political-ethical understanding about, violations of human rights and mass criminality that were planned, executed, and passively supported or tolerated by others within a national framework. From this viewpoint, Goldhagen's methodological approach emerges as a genuine philosophical contribution as well. He employs an interpretive framework that allows him to introduce the moral dimension – the freedom to act – into the historical analysis of directly involved perpetrators. "Freedom" in this sense is what we attribute to an agent who has acted accountably, with the knowledge of other alternatives to the given action, and who considers his action to be normatively justified.

2 This text served as preparation for a conversation with Gerhard Schröder, which took place on June 5, 1998 as part of the Cultural Forum of the SPD.

Chapter 1   What is a People?

1   J.D. Sauerländers Verlag, Frankfurt/M. 1847. (Hereafter cited as *"Proceedings."*)
2   Ibid. 6.
3   E. Rothacker, *Logik und Systematik der Geisteswissenschaften*, Bonn 1948, 116.
4   U. Mewes, "Zur Namengebung 'Germanistik,'" in J. Fohrmannn and W. Voßkamp (eds), *Wissenschaftsgeschichte der Germanistik im 19. Jahrhundert*, Stuttgart and Weimar 1994, 25–47.
5   J.J. Müller, "Die erste Germanistentage," in J.J. Müller (ed.), *Literaturwissenschaft und Sozialwissenschaften*, vol. 2, Stuttgart 1974, 297–318.
6   *Proceedings*, 62.
7   Ibid. 60.
8   Ibid.
9   Ibid. 62.
10   Ibid. 11.
11   Ibid. 115
12   Ibid. 119.
13   Ibid. 17.
14   Ibid. 11.
15   Wilhelm Scherer, *Vorträge und Aufsätze*, Berlin 1874, 340f. (Quoted in Rothacker [see n. 3], 119.
16   *Proceedings*, 61.
17   Ibid. 113.
18   Ibid. 107.
19   Ibid. 13.
20   Ibid.: "Since Luther, the dominance of the High German dialect has been irrevocably established, and the regions of Germany are now willing to lay down the particular advantages that each familiar dialect carries with it, if by doing so they increase the force and the strength of the communal and noble written language arising in them all."
21   "It is a sin to employ foreign words where comparable or even better German words are available." Ibid. 14.
22   Ibid. 123.
23   Ibid. 68.
24   As in the title of the programmatic work by Georg Beseler of 1843.

25 G. Dilcher and B.R. Kern, "Die juristische Germanistik des 19. Jahrhunderts und die Fachtradition der deutschen Rechtsgeschichte," *Zeitschrift für Rechtsgeschichte*, CXIV Band, Germ. Abt. (1984), 1–46.

26 *Proceedings*, 151.

27 Ibid. 82.

28 Ibid. 73 f.

29 Ibid. 149.

30 Ibid. 100: "Where republics, constitutional states, and absolute monarchies are unified in one federation, one cannot of course speak of an encompassing legislation. But there still remains the great range of private or civil legislation, and criminal law."

31 Ibid. 84.

32 Ibid. 124 ff.

33 *Heidelberger Jahrbücher der Literatur* 26 (1833), 555.

34 P.U. Hohendahl, *Literarische Kultur im Zeitalter des Liberalismus 1830–1870*, Munich 1985, chs VI and VII.

35 W. Boehlich (ed.), *Der Hochverratsprozeß gegen Gervinus*, Frankfurt/M. 1967.

36 G.C. Gervinus, *Einleitung in die Geschichte des neunzehnten Jahrhunderts*, ed. W. Boehlich, Frankfurt/M. 1967, 153, 162.

37 Ibid. 150.

38 Ibid. 166.

39 Ibid. 135.

40 J. Fröbel, *System der sozialen Politik* (2nd edn, Mannheim 1847), reprinted Aalen 1975, vol. I, 242 ff.

41 Ibid. 245.

42 From this point of view, moreover, Fröbel criticizes the principle of international law that forbids intervention in the internal affairs of other states even in 1847, and argues for humanitarian interventions. See ibid. 250.

43 T. Parsons and G.M. Platt, *The American University*, Cambridge, MA, 1973, 90 ff.

44 K. Weimar, *Geschichte der deutschen Literaturwissenschaft bis zum Ende des 19. Jahrhunderts*, Munich 1989; U. Hunger, "Die altdeutsche Literatur und das Verlangen nach Wissenschaft," in Fohrmann and Voßkamp (see n. 4), 236–63.

45 R. Kolk, "Liebhaber, Gelehrte, Experten," in Fohrmann and Voßkamp (see n. 4), 84–7; on the development of the discipline from its romantic beginnings to the "esoteric elitist discipline," see R. Krohn, "Die Altergermanistik des 19. Jahrhunderts und

ihre Wege in die Öffentlichkeit," in Fohrmann and Voßkamp (see n. 4), 264–333.

46 Weimar (see n. 44), 319–46.

47 D. Kopp, "Deutsche Philologie und Erziehungssystem," in Fohrmann and Voßkamp, (see n. 4), 669–741.

48 Ibid. 705.

49 A. Assmann, *Die Arbeit am nationalen Gedächtnis*, Frankfurt/M. 1993, 61.

50 N. Wegmann, "Was heißt einen 'klassischen Text' lesen? Philologische Selbstreflexion zwischen Wissenschaft und Bildung," in Fohrmann and Voßkamp (see n. 4), 334–50.

51 Thus according to Gadamer in *Truth and Method*, New York 1975: "The classical is what resists historical criticism because its historical dominion, the binding power of its validity that is preserved and handed down, precedes all historical reflection and continues through it."

52 Kopp (see n. 47), 725.

53 Assmann (see n. 49), 46.

54 F. Trommler, "Germanistik und Öffentlichkeit," in Ch. König and E. Lämmert (eds), *Literaturwissenschaft und Geistesgeschichte*, Frankfurt/M. 1993, 307–30.

55 W. Voßkamp, "Literatursoziologie: Eine Alternative zur Geistesgeschichte?", in König and Lämmert (see n. 54), 291–303.

56 Leo Löwenthal, "Zur gesellschaftlichen Lage der Literatur," *Zeitschrift für Sozialforschung* I (1932), 85–102, here 87.

57 T.W. Adorno, *Notes to Literature*, ed. Rolf Tiedemann, New York 1991.

58 "There is no art that does not contain in itself as an element, negated, what it repulses." Theodor W. Adomo, *Aesthetic Theory*, tr. Robert Hullot-Kentor, Minneapolis 1997, 11.

Chapter 2   On the Public Use of History

1 This text is based on the honorary address that I delivered at the award ceremony on March 10, 1997.

2 Daniel Goldhagen, *Hitler's Willing Executioners: Ordinary Germans and the Holocaust*, New York 1996.

3 H. Jäger, who himself published an early study of criminal violence in the Nazi regime, emphasizes that Goldhagen's book does not argue for collective guilt, as it is often accused of doing; rather the book "reveals a massive individual guilt."

"Die Widerlegung des funktionalistisches Täterbildes," *Mittelweg* 36 (February/March 1997).

4 Dieter Pohl, "Die Holocaust-Forschung und Goldhagens Thesen," *Vierteljahreshefte für Zeitgeschichte* (1997), 1–48.
5 Goldhagen (see n. 2), 318.
6 Christopher Browning, *Ordinary Men*, New York 1992.
7 Goldhagen (see n. 2), 22.
8 J. H. Schoeps, *Ein Volk von Mördern?*, Heidelberg 1996.
9 Goldhagen (see n. 2), 430–1.
10 Ibid. 425.
11 D. Goldhagen, *Hitlers Willige Vorstrecker*, Berlin 1996, 8.
12 Ian Kershaw, *The Nazi Dictatorship: Problems and Perspectives of Interpretation*, London 1993.

Chapter 3   Learning from Catastrophe?

1 Eric Hobsbawm, *The Age of Extremes: A History of the World 1914–1991*, New York 1994. I owe more to this stimulating book than the notes express.
2 Ibid. 558–9.
3 W. Heitmeyer (ed.), *Was treibt die Gesellschaft auseinander?*, Frankfurt/M. 1997.
4 N. Luhmann, "Jenseits von Barbarei," in M. Miller and H.G. Soeffner (eds.), *Modernität und Barbarei*, Frankfurt/M. 1996, 219–30.
5 R. Dahrendorf describes this in "Squaring the Circle," *Transit* 12 (1996), 5–28.
6 My thanks for permission to look at the following manuscripts: C. Offe, "Precariousness and the Labor Market. A Medium Term Review of Available Policy Responses" (MS 1997); J. Neyer and M. Seeleib-Kaiser, "Bringing Economy Back," in *Economic Globalization and the Re-commodification of the Workforce*, Zentrum für Sozialpolitik, University of Bremen, working paper 16/1995; H. Wiesenthal, "Globalisierung. Soziologische und politikwissenschaftliche Koordinaten eines unbekannten Territoriums" (MS 1995).
7 The following receives a fuller treatment in J. Habermas, "Jenseits des Nationalstaates? Zu einigen Folgeproblemen der wirtschaftlichen Globalisierung," in U. Beck (ed.), *Politik der Globalisierung*, Frankfurt/M. 1998, 67–84.
8 See pp. 89–100.

9 D. Senghaas, "Interdependenzen im internationalen System," in G. Krell and H. Müller (eds), *Frieden und Konflikt in den internationalen Beziehungen*, Frankfurt/M. 1994, 190–222.

10 I do not believe that the unpredictable implosion of the Soviet Union has discredited my diagnosis from 1985: J. Habermas, "The New Obscurity and the Exhaustion of Utopian Energies," in Shierry Weber Nicholson (ed. and tr.), *The New Conservatism: Cultural Criticism and the Historians' Debate*, Cambridge, MA, 1989.

11 D. Held, *Democracy and the Global Order*, Cambridge 1995.

12 U. Beck, *Gegengifte. Die organisierte Unverantwortlichkeit*, Frankfurt/M. 1988.

13 On the model of a global domestic policy without global governance, cf. pp. 100–12.

Chapter 4   The Postnational Constellation and the Future of Democracy

1 Siegfried Landshut, *Kritik der Soziologie*, Neuwied 1969, 85.

2 U. Menzel, *Globalisierung vs. Fragmentierung*, Frankfurt/M. 1998.

3 John Rawls, *A Theory of Justice*, Cambridge, MA 1971.

4 Ulrich Beck, "Wie wird Demokratie im Zeitalter der Globalisierung möglich?", in Beck (ed.), *Politik der Globalisierung*, Frankfurt/M. 1998, introduction, 7–66. My thanks to Ulrich Beck for additional references.

5 A. McGrew, "Globalization and Territorial Democracy," in McGrew (ed.), *The Transformation of Democracy?*, Cambridge 1997, 12.

6 On following see J. Habermas, "The European Nation- State: On the Past and Future of Sovereignty and Citizenship," in Ciaran Cronin and Pablo de Greiff (eds), *The Inclusion of the Other*, Cambridge, MA 1998, 105–28.

7 J. Habermas, *Between Facts and Norms: Contributions to a Discourse Theory of Law and Democracy*, tr. William Rehg, Cambridge, MA 1996, 132ff.

8 R. Alexy, *Theorie der Grundrechte*, Frankfurt/M. 1986, 378ff.

9 U. Beck, *What is Globalization?*, Cambridge 2000.

10 J. Perraton, D. Goldblatt, D. Held and A. McGrew, "Die Globalisierung der Wirtschaft," in: Beck (see n. 4), 134–68; here 167; cf. also D. Held, "Democracy and Globalization," in *Global Governance* 3 (1997), 251–67. More specific is W. Streek,

"Industrielle Beziehungen in einer institutionalisierten Wirtschaft," in Beck (see n. 4), 169–202, here 176f.

11 R. Cox, "Democracy in Hard Times," in McGrew (see n. 5), 55.

12 In this sense, John Agnew and Stuart Corbridge associate "the trend from boundary to flow" with these developments; see Agnew and Corbridge, *Mastering Space*, London 1995, 216. The other image, "from barriers to (video) screens," alludes to the virtualization of borders.

13 Menzel (see n. 2), 15.

14 Cox (see n. 11), 51.

15 On the following, cf. M. Zürn, *Regieren jenseits des National-staates*, Frankfurt/M. 1998.

16 U. Beck, *Risikogesellschaft*, Frankfurt/M. 1986.

17 Commission on the Future of the Friedrich-Ebert Foundation (eds.), *Wirtschaftliche Leistungsfähigkeit, sozialer Zusammenhalt und ökologische Nachhaltigkeit*, Bonn 1998, 204–22.

18 Cf. the definitive works by H.J. Morgenthau, *Politics among Nations*, New York 1949, and K.E. Waltz, *Man, the State, and War*, New York 1959.

19 R.O. Keohane, *After Hegemony: Cooperation and Discord in the World Political Economy*, Princeton 1984.

20 E.O. Czempiel, *Weltpolitik im Umbruch*, Munich 1993; S. Laubach-Hintermeier, "Kritik des Realismus," in C. Chwaszcza and W. Kersting (eds), *Politische Philosophie der internationalen Beziehungen*, Frankfurt/M. 1998, 73–95.

21 D. Held, "Democracy, the Nation State and the Global System," in Held (ed.), *Political Theory Today*, Cambridge 1991, 197–235, here 201ff.

22 Agnew and Corbridge (see n. 12), 94.

23 Cf. Zürn (see n. 15).

24 M. Imber, "Geo-Governance without Democracy," in McGrew (see n. 5), 201ff.

25 A. Margalit and J. Raz, "National Self-Determination," in W. Kymlicka (ed.), *The Rights of Minority Cultures*, Oxford 1995, 79–92; A. Buchanan, "The Morality of Secession," in Kymlicka, 350–74.

26 J. Habermas, "The Asylum Debate," in Max Pensky (ed.), *The Past as Future*, Lincoln, NE 1994, 121–42.

27 C. Offe, "'Homogeneity' and Constitutional Democracy," *The Journal of Political Philosophy* 6:2 (1998), 113–41.

28 J. Habermas, "Inklusion – Einbeziehen oder Einschließen?" in Habermas, *Die Einbeziehung des Anderen*, Frankfurt/M. 1996, 154–84.

29 W. Kymlicka, *Multicultural Citizenship*, Oxford 1995.

30 A. Margalit and M. Halbertal, "Liberalism and the Right to Culture," *Social Research* (1993), 491–510, here 507. The same attitude toward cultural resources is justified on the intrinsic basis of preserving one's own identity, and not, as some liberal theorists suggest, instrumentally – as a sort of warehouse of values from which private autonomous decision-makers can satisfy their higher-order preferences; cf. J. Raz, "Multiculturalism: A Liberal Perspective," *Dissent* (Winter 1994), 67–79.

31 Cf. my interview with J.M. Ferry in J. Habermas, *Die nachholende Revolution*, Frankfurt/M. 1990, 149–56, here 153ff.

32 D. Miller, *Worlds Apart: Modernity through the Prism of the Local*, London 1995, "Introduction: Anthropology, Modernity, and Consumption," 1–22.

33 Cf. the contributions in Miller (see n. 32).

34 G. Baumann, *Contesting Culture: Discourses of Identity in Multi-Ethnic London*, Cambridge 1996.

35 J. Waldron, "Minority Cultures and the Cosmopolitan Alternative," in Kymlicka (see n. 25), 105:

> The cosmopolitan strategy is not to deny the role of culture in the constitution of human life, but to question, first, the assumption that the social world divides up neatly into particular distinct cultures, one to every community, and secondly, the assumption that what everyone needs is just one of these entities – a single, coherent culture – to give shape and meaning to his life.

36 D. Oberndörfer, "Integration oder Abschottung?", *Zeitschrift für Ausländerrecht und Ausländerpolitik* 18 (January 1998), 3–13.

37 Cf. my response to R. Bernstein in Habermas (see n. 28), 310ff.

38 R.W. Cox, "Global Restructuring: Making Sense of the Changing International Economy," in R. Stubbs and G. Underhill (eds), *Political Economy and the Changing Global Order*, New York 1994, 45–59.

39 Agnew and Corbridge (see n. 12), 164–210.

40 E. Helleiner, "From Bretton Woods to Global Finance," in Stubbs and Underhill (see n. 38), 163–75.

41 J. Neyer, *Spiel ohne Grenzen*, Marburg 1996.

42 On the problems arising from local competition cf. F.W. Scharpf, "Demokratie in der transnationalen Politik," in Beck (see n. 4), 228–53, here 243ff.

43 R. Dahrendorf, "Die Quadratur des Kreises," *Transit* 12 (Winter 1996), 5–28, here 9.

44 Typical is M. Albrow, *Abschied vom Nationalstaat*, Frankfurt/M. 1998.

45 Pierre Bourdieu follows the same strategy with the thesis:

> One can argue against the nation-state and nevertheless defend its "universal" functions, which can be fulfilled just as well, if not better, by a supranational state. If one doesn't want the Bundesbank to use its interest rate policies to determine the economic features of individual states, then mustn't one advocate the creation of a supranational state that would be relatively independent from international economic and political forces, and that would be in a position to develop the social dimension of European institutions? (P. Bourdieu, "Der Mythos 'Globalisierung' und der europäische Sozialstaat," in Bourdieu, *Gegenfeuer*, Constance 1998, 49 f)

46 On the forms of social integration and the differentiation of networks and corporative entities cf. B. Peters, *Die Integration moderner Gesellschaften*, Frankfurt/M. 1993, 96 ff and 165 ff.

47 J. Habermas, *The Philosophical Discourse of Modernity*, tr. Frederick Lawrence, Cambridge, MA 1987, ch. 12.

48 K. Polanyi, *The Great Transformation*, Frankfurt/M. 1978, 333.

49 Cox, in McGrew (see n. 5), 53 f.

50 J. Habermas, "Was heißt Sozialismus heute?" in Habermas (see n. 31), 194 f.

51 P. Wagner, *Soziologie der Moderne*, Frankfurt/M. 1995, 180.

52 See U. Beck (see n. 16); also U. Beck, A. Giddens, and S. Lash, *Reflexive Modernisierung*, Frankfurt/M. 1996.

53 U. Beck, *Gegengifte: Die organisierte Unverantwortlichkeit*, Frankfurt/M. 1988; U. Beck (ed.), *Kinder der Freiheit*, Frankfurt/M. 1997.

54 W. Heitmeyer (ed.), *Was treibt die Gesellschaft auseinander?*, Frankfurt/M. 1997.

55 Wagner (see n. 51), 261.

56 J.M. Guéhenno, *Das Ende der Demokratie*, Munich and Zurich 1994.

57　E. Grande, "Postnationale Demokratie – ein Ausweg aus der Globalisierungsfalle?," in W. Fricke and E. Fricke (eds), *Jahrbuch für Arbeit und Technik*, Bonn 1997, 353–67.

58　Commission on the Future of the Friedrich-Ebert Foundation (see n. 17), 225 ff.

59　G. Grözinger, "Drei wirtschaftspolitische Ziele, drei semi-autonome Institutionen," in *Wirtschaftswissenschaftliche Diskussionsbeiträge* Nr. 8. Flensburg 1998.

60　Scharpf (see n. 42), 247 ff.

61　What G. Voruba ("Ende der Vollbeschäftigungsgesellschaft," *Zeitschrift für Sozialreform* 44 (1998), 77–99) says concerning the idea of shareholder socialism can be meaningfully related to another plane of the – equalizing – combination of several sources of income:

All these approaches move beyond releasing previous assignations of population groups to income sources and interest positions. More simply: if capitalism has triumphed, then everyone has to be turned into (partial) capitalists to be able to share in the fruits of this victory. If conditional employment no longer is adequate as an income source, it has to be increased via capital income.

62　Agnew and Corbridge (see n. 12), 201 f.

63　Ibid. 222 f.

64　J.R. Hollingsworth and R. Boyer, *Contemporary Capitalism*, Cambridge 1997, 1–48.

65　Ibid. 37.

66　Commission on the Future of the Friedrich-Ebert Foundation (see n. 17), 76 ff.

67　F.W. Scharpf, *Optionen des Föderalismus in Deutschland und Europa*, Frankfurt/M. 1994.

68　St. Leibfried and P. Pierson (eds), *Standort Europa: Europäische Sozialpolitik*, Frankfurt/M. 1998.

69　Grözinger (see n. 59).

70　W. Streeck, "Vom Binnenmarkt zum Bundesstaat? Überlegungen zur politischen Ökonomie der europäischen Sozialpolitik," in Leibfried and Pierson (see n. 68), 377 ff.

71　P. Pierson and St. Leibfried, "Zur Dynamik sozialpolitischer Integration: Der Wohlfahrtsstaat in der europäischen Mehrebenenpolitik, in Leibfried and Pierson (see n. 68), 425 ff.

72　Streeck (see n. 70), 391.

73   C. Offe, "Demokratie und Wohlfartsstaat," (MS 1998), 27.

74   Ibid. 22.

75   E. Grande, "Demokratische Legitimation und europäische Integration," *Leviathan* 1996, 339–60; R. Schmalz-Bruns, "Bürgergesellschaftliche Politik – ein Modell der Demokratisierung der Europäischen Union," in K.D. Wolf (ed.), *Projekt Europa im Übergang?*, Baden-Baden 1997, 63–90.

76   D. Grimm, *Braucht Europa eine Verfassung?* (Carl Friedrich von Siemens Stiftung), Munich 1995.

77   Cf. my comments on Grimm in Habermas (see n. 6), 155 ff; cf. also G. Delanty, "Models of Citizenship: Defining European Identity and Citizenship," *Citizenship Studies* 1 (1997), 285–304.

78   Offe (see n. 73), 46.

79   E.W. Böckenförde, *Welchen Weg geht Europa?* (Carl Friedrich von Siemens Stiftung), Munich 1997, 37.

80   The impulses of the Left toward such a discussion are rather weak; cf. P. Gowan and P. Anderson (eds), *The Question of Europe*, London 1997.

81   S. Sassen, *Globalization and its Discontents*, New York 1998, 199.

82   Cf. Sassen (ibid. 202 f):

> A focus on place, and particularly the type of place I call "global cities," brings to the fore the fact that many of the resources necessary for global economic activities are not hypermobile and could, in principle, be brought under effective regulation... A refocussing of regulation onto infrastructures and production complexes in the context of globalization contributes to an analysis of the regulatory capacities of states that diverges in significant ways from understandings centered on hypermobile outputs and global telecommunications.

83   D. Archigubi, "Models of International Organization in Perpetual Peace Projects," *Review of International Studies* 18 (1992), 295–317.

84   D. Held, *Democracy and the Global Order*, Cambridge 1995, 267–87.

85   D. Archigubi, "From the United Nations to Cosmopolitan Democracy," in D. Archigubi and D. Held (eds), *Cosmopolitan Democracy: An Agenda for a New World Order*, Cambridge 1995, 121–62; D. Held, "Democracy and the New World Order," ibid. 96–120.

86 Cosmopolitan consciousness could in any case take on a more concrete form by a delimitation of the temporal dimension – a stylization of the resistance of the present to the past of the nation-state.

87 Habermas (see n. 6), 220–6.

88 C. Taylor, "A World Consensus on Human Rights?" *Dissent* (Summer 1996), 15–21; J. Habermas, "Remarks on Legitimization through Human Rights," *Philosophy and Social Criticism* 24 (1998), 157–72; on this see also T. McCarthy, "On Reconciling Cosmopolitan Unity and National Diversity" (MS 1998).

89 J. Habermas, "Three Normative Models of Democracy," in Habermas (see n. 6), 239–52.

90 A. Linklater, "Cosmopolitan Citizenship," *Citizenship Studies* 2 (1998), 23–41.

91 Jamie Carney, "Structure for a Democratic World Government" (MS 1998).

Chapter 5 Remarks on Legitimation through Human Rights

1 J. Habermas, *Between Facts and Norms: Contributions to a Discourse Theory of Law and Democracy*, tr. William Rehg, Cambridge, MA 1996, ch. 3.

2 I. Maus, "Die Trennung von Recht und Moral als Begrenzung des Rechts," in Maus, *Zur Aufklärung der Demokratietheorie*, Frankfurt/M. 1992, 308–36.

3 On the following cf. J. Habermas, "On the Internal Relation between the Rule of Law and Democracy," in Habermas, *The Inclusion of the Other. Studies in Political Theory*, Cambridge 1998, 253–64; I cannot here go into the friendly criticism of Ingeborg Maus' *Freiheitsrechte und Volkssouveranität*, in *Rechtstheorie* 26 (1995), 507–62.

4 R. Herzog ("Die Rechte des Menschen," *Die Zeit*, September 6, 1996) of course rightly distinguishes between the founding and the realization of human rights.

5 I. Maus, "Volkssouveranität und das Prinzip Nichtintervention in der Friedensphilosophie Immanuel Kants," in H. Brunkhorst (ed.), *Einmischung erwünscht?*, Frankfurt/M. 88–116.

6 L. Wingert, "Türöffner zu geschlossenen Gesellschaften," *Frankfurter Rundschau*, August 6, 1995.

7 For a comprehensive criticism of Carl Schmitt's legal theory
   cf. I. Maus, *Bürgerliche Rechtstheorie und Faschismus*, Munich
   1980.
8 Cf. the parallel position of the Nigerian political scientist Claude
   Ake, in "The African Context of Human Rights," *Africa Today*
   34 (1987), 5:

The idea of human rights, or legal rights in general, presupposes a
society which is atomized and individualistic, a society of en-
demic conflict. It presupposes a society of people conscious of
their separatedness and their particular interests and anxious to
realize them . . . We put less emphasis on the individual and more
on the collectivity, we do not allow that the individual has any
claims which may override that of the society. We assume har-
mony, not divergence of interests, competition and conflict; we
are more inclined to think of our obligations to other members of
our society rather than of our claims against them.

 9 Yash Ghai, "Human Rights and Governance: The Asia Debate,"
    Center for Asian Pacific Affairs (November 1994), 1–19.
10 Cf. my disagreement with Günther Frankenberg, in Habermas,
    Die Einbeziehung des Anderen, Frankfurt/M. 1996, 382 ff.
11 Ghai (see n. 9), 10:

Governments have destroyed many communities in the name of
development or state stability, and the consistent refusal of most
of them to recognize that there are indigenous people among
their population who have a right to preserve their traditional
culture, economy and beliefs, is but a demonstration of their lack
of commitment to the real community. The vitality of the community comes from the exercise of rights to organize, meet,
debate, and protest, dismissed as "liberal" rights by these governments.

12 Partha Chatterjee, "Secularism and Toleration," *Economic and
    Political Weekly*, July 9, 1994, 1768–76; Rajeev Bhargava, "Giv-
    ing Secularism its Due," *Economic and Political Weekly*, July 9,
    1994, 1784–91.
13 H. Hoibraaten, "Secular Society," in T. Lindholm and K. Vogt
    (eds), *Islamic Law Reform and Human Rights*, Oslo 1993, 231–57.
14 John Rawls, *Political Liberalism*, New York 1993.

Chapter 6　Conceptions of Modernity

1　Lecture for the Korean Society for Philosophy, Seoul, May 1996.
2　H.R. Jauss, *Literaturgeschichte als Provokation*, Frankfurt/M. 1970, 11.
3　J. Habermas, *The Philosophical Discourse of Modernity*, tr. Frederick Lawrence, Cambridge, MA 1987, 23–43.
4　R. Koselleck, *Futures Past: On the Semantics of Historical Time*, Cambridge, MA 1987.
5　G.W.F. Hegel, *Werke*, Frankfurt/M. 1986, vol. 20, 329.
6　Cf. The dissertation of the same title by R. Koselleck, *Kritik und Krise: Eine Studie zur Pathogenese der bürgerlichen Welt*, Freiburg 1959.
7　Cf. Th. M. Schmidt, *Anerkennung und absolute Religion*, Stuttgart 1997.
8　S. Landshut, "Kritik der Soziologie. Freiheit und Gleichheit als Ursprungsproblem der Soziologie," in Landshut, *Kritik der Soziologie*, Neuwied 1969.
9　H. Marcuse, *Reason and Revolution*, Boston 1969. Classical social theories can be understood as responses to the crisis tendencies of their time; on this cf. J. Habermas, "Kritische und konservative Aufgaben der Soziologie," in Habermas, *Theorie und Praxis*, Frankfurt/M. 1971, 290–306; see also my treatment of sociology in the Weimar Republic in Habermas, *Texte und Kontexte*, Frankfurt/M. 1991, 184–204.
10　For a more exhaustive treatment of Weber's diagnosis of his times, which is highly simplified in what follows here, see Habermas, *Theory of Communicative Action*, Boston 1981, vol. I, 143–243.
11　Ibid. 339–402.
12　C. Lafont, *Sprache und Welterschließung*, Frankfurt/M. 1994.
13　Karl-Otto Apel recognized this very early, in 1962 in his inaugural lecture on Wittgenstein and Heidegger at Kiel University; cf. Apel, *Transformation of Philosophy*, vol. I, Frankfurt/M. 1973, 225–75.
14　P. Wagner, *Soziologie der Moderne*, Frankfurt/M. 1995.
15　Cf. R. Bernstein, *Beyond Objectivity and Relativism*, Philadelphia 1983, 51–108.
16　R. Rorty, *Objectivity, Relativism, and Truth: Philosophical Papers*, vol. I, Cambridge 1991, 21 ff.

17 J. Habermas, *Nachmetaphysisches Denken*, Frankfurt/M. 1988, 175–9.
18 Habermas (see n. 10), vol. II, 113 ff.
19 A. Honneth (ed.), *Pathologien des Sozialen*, Frankfurt/M. 1994.
20 U. Beck, *Risk Society: towards a new modernity*, London 1992. Frankfurt/M. 1986.
21 U. Beck, in U. Beck, A. Giddens, and S. Lash, *Reflexive Modernization: Politics, Tradition, and Aesthetics in the Modern Social Order*, Cambridge 1994.
22 J. Habermas, *Between Facts and Norms: Contributions to a Discourse Theory of Law and Democracy*, tr. William Rehg, Cambridge, MIT Press, 1996.
23 J. Habermas, "Individuierung durch Vergesellschaftung," in Habermas (see n. 17), 234 ff.

Chapter 8   An Argument against Human Cloning

1 In *Süddeutsche Zeitung*, January 13, 1998.
2 Published in *Die Zeit*, February 19, 1998.
3 In *Die Zeit*, February 12, 1998.
4 Published in *Die Zeit*, March 12, 1998.
5 In *Die Zeit*, March 5, 1998.

Index